Jesus,
KEEPER OF MY HEART

POETRY, DEVOTIONALS AND TESTIMONIES ABOUT
JESUS' LOVE FOR HIS CHILDREN

Donna McMillin

WESTBOW
PRESS®
A DIVISION OF THOMAS NELSON
& ZONDERVAN

WestBow Press books may be ordered through booksellers or by contacting:

WestBow Press
A Division of Thomas Nelson & Zondervan
1663 Liberty Drive
Bloomington, IN 47403
www.westbowpress.com
844-714-3454

ISBN: 979-8-3850-3818-3 (sc)
ISBN: 979-8-3850-3820-6 (hc)
ISBN: 979-8-3850-3819-0 (e)

Library of Congress Control Number: 2024925495

Print information available on the last page.

WestBow Press rev. date: 01/09/2025

"In memory of our beloved brother, Mike, whom we love so very much and will miss greatly until we see you again in our heavenly home with Jesus."

DEDICATION

I dedicate this book to my heavenly Father, God, and Savior, Jesus Christ, who has been better to me than ten sons. He has poured out His everlasting love in my heart, overflowing from the first day I found and accepted His offer of forgiveness, cleansing, peace, mercy, grace, and abundant life. God is always faithful, even when we are not faithful. He is worthy of all our trust, as He cares so greatly for us. In loving us, He sent His Only Begotten Son, Jesus, to die for our sins to redeem us back to our Father in heaven. What love we cannot yet grasp all of it, but one day soon, we will look upon our Savior's face and see all His love poured out on us and so much more.

Also, I dedicate this book to my wonderful husband, Jim, who the Lord gifted me with as the love of my earthly life. He, too, has been better to me than ten sons, just as God promised me years ago in a dream. I love this man of mine more with every passing day we spend together on this earth and feel so blessed to call him my husband. He has supported me and worked hard all our marriage and loved me thoroughly and unconditionally. He is such a patient and giving man. My heavenly Father knew whom I needed in this life to help keep me grounded and stable in my walk with Him. I love you, Jim. I am forever blessed to not only spend this life with you but to know we will be together forever in eternity with our Savior, Jesus Christ.

I thank my beautiful, godly sisters for taking part in this to share their love of Jesus and how He made a difference in their lives. Thank you for all your prayers and support for this book. Iron sharpening iron we have been to each other through these years. I love you all so much. Thank you for praying me into the kingdom of God and for being the mighty prayer warriors you are. Each time I reach out to you all to pray for one thing or another, you are all always faithful to lift each situation to the throne of our mighty God.

I thank both families (Boyd and McMillin), church family, and friends who have prayed for and supported this endeavor, and for all your encouragement to me in following the Lord's prompting to put this book together to glorify Him. Many thanks to my pastors, Mike and Cathy Posey, for all your prayers, encouragement, support, and for believing in me. I especially thank you, Pastor Mike, for allowing me times to speak my poems to our people at church. I pray you all will be blessed by this book that I believe is from God's heart to mine.

A special thanks to Michelle Posey, who agreed to proofread this book for me. Not only did I receive that gift from her, she also gave some great insight into how I could improve the wording in some of the poems. Her help greatly aided in finally getting this book into the hands of people like you. Thank you, Michelle, for always using the great creativity gift God gave you for His glory and to help others.

Also, a special thanks to Daneilya Austin for the beautiful cover she created from a dream I had. When I first saw the cover, it took my breath away. I am surrounded by talented godly women who surprise me at every turn.

CONTENTS

FOREWORDS

I have known Donna for over twenty years. In that time, I have found her to be a woman of conviction, passion, compassion, a committed learner, and a loyal friend. These qualities are rooted in her desire to please Jesus. Recently, she has gone public in expressing these attributes in poetry. Many of her poems are weighty and will bring affirmation as well as personal examination. At the core of her poems, the glory of God is being revealed in the earth and in us.

There is a phrase in the Bible that declares, "We are God's workmanship, created in Christ Jesus for good works" (Ephesians 2:10). The word for "workmanship" has been translated as a "masterpiece" or "poem." In this book of poetry, you will become more aware that you are God's masterpiece and His poem. It has been my honor to walk with Donna and witness her continual growth and transformation as she strives to walk in the good works that God has ordained for her. As you read and meditate on her poetry, your eyes will awaken to how glorious our God truly is.

Apostle Michael Posey, Lead Pastor,
The Dwelling Place Church, Evansville, Indiana

I've had the pleasure of serving and worshipping with Donna and her husband, Jim, for approximately twenty years and an even greater pleasure in calling them friends. During that time, I've witnessed in Donna a servant's heart, an unwavering faith in Christ, a deep love of the scriptures, and a passion for sharing her faith with others. It was with surprise and delight that Donna recently began to share her poetry with me that she had been writing and collecting for many years and recently had intensified. Her poems will inspire your faith and take you on a journey from celebration to contemplation. They will move your heart to go deeper in your relationship with the Lord Jesus. Her poetry can be enjoyed by all ages and, much like the hymns of old, are rich with scriptural themes that will impart knowledge to the reader.

Jeff Biggerstaff, Assistant Pastor,
The Dwelling Place Church, Evansville, Indiana

At times, life affects and even infects us—all of us—and we need encouragement. This book is just what Jesus, the Master Physician, ordered, a prescription for encouragement as you flesh out your own personal journey of faith.

We have known the author, Donna McMillin, for over twenty years and have watched her grow in grace and wisdom as she embraced her God-calling. This book, *Jesus, Keeper of My Heart*, is a culmination of many years of faithful servanthood to the Lord and His people. We highly recommend this compilation of God thoughts poured out and penned from a caring, honest, sincere, and heartfelt love for God's people. You will be blessed. Reading it once will never be enough. It will become your survival guide second only to the scriptures. Be encouraged, and stay the course through all those tough times. Please know that the best is yet to come!

Dan and Sue Caldwell
Smithy Ministries International

PREFACE

These are poems I have written to the Lord since I gave my heart to Jesus in January 1988 and then baptized in February 1988.

In 1987, I was in the US Marine Corps, stationed in Nashville, Tennessee, at the I&I Reserve Duty Station. A coworker and his wife invited me to their house for a New Year's Eve party. But one day, he came to me and said his party was canceled because he had given his life to the Lord. And from that day on, he continually asked me to go to church with him and his wife. I always said no and that the church would probably fall in if I went to church. Finally, I got so tired of him asking, I gave in and accepted his invitation. But I told him he better be at the door at exactly 10 a.m., the time church service started, or I would leave.

So, that Sunday I pulled into the parking lot listening to my secular music and parked the car. I kept a keen eye on my watch for the time; I meant what I said about exactly 10 a.m. It seemed like the minutes and seconds barely ticked by, but finally, my watch showed 10 a.m. I didn't see him out in the front, so I reached down to restart the car. And, lo and behold, he walked out the door and saw me. I was thinking about how close I came to being able to leave. But I kept my word, as he kept his, and walked inside church. The walls did not cave in. Thankfully!

I sat in a pew with him and other coworkers. For the life of me, I couldn't tell you what the preacher preached that day. All I could hear was my heavenly Father speaking directly to my heart, letting me experience a love I had longed for all my life but never found in the things I was doing. A love that was lifting shame and guilt off my shoulders, restoring my brokenness, and giving me the opportunity for a new life in Him. I cried my eyes out that day, emptying my heart out to Him, and I didn't even really understand all that was going on. The sin, shame, and guilt I had carried since I was fifteen years old was lifted off my shoulders by nothing I was doing but by a loving Savior, Jesus Christ. He poured out His love, mercy, and grace to me that day and stretched out His hand for me to take.

Oh, you better believe I took His hand and all He offered me that day. He washed my sins away, and He came into my heart to live.

I truly did not understand all that was happening at the time. All I knew is I walked in a sinner burdened with shame and walked out knowing in my heart I was never going back to that life again. Never! That day, Jesus delivered me from drug and alcohol addiction, and in the thirty-six years since, I have never consumed either again. He washed me white as snow.

Jesus gave me a new life on that day in January 1988. A new person in Jesus Christ, my heart was changed from the inside out, and I knew I would never be the same again. That day I walked out of church free of all addictions and sin and free to live for Jesus forever with the promise of eternal life through faith in Jesus Christ as the Son of God. He died on the cross for my sins and the sins of the world, was buried, rose on the third day, and is seated at the right hand of God the Father. Hallelujah! I was born again by the Holy Spirit of God and raised to life in Jesus.

When I first got saved, I couldn't wait to get home after work to read my Bible and see what God was speaking to me. I remember first reading the book of Daniel and loving it. The courage of Daniel, and the three Hebrew boys, Hananiah (Shadrach), Mishael (Meshach), and Azariah (Abednego), oh my goodness, I couldn't get enough. My heart yearned for all the truth and stories of those who had been before us in the biblical times. Reading and experiencing God as I read His Word every night was exciting and real in my heart to my very soul. It was like God was downloading His Word into my heart, like He was writing His Word on my heart and searing it into me. I loved every bit of my time in the Word of God and in His presence. And I still do.

In this collection of poems, you will see my heart's cries, my ups and downs, my highs and lows, my struggles and failures, and my victories in Jesus. I hope you will be able to see yourself in them and know that you, too, will have victory over all that you are or will go through in life. I am still growing every day in His love and truth, staying in His Word and in His presence, worshipping Him, and opening my heart to Jesus, the author and finisher of my faith.

My prayer is that our God and Savior, Jesus Christ, will touch your heart with the poems He put in my heart to Him, and you will experience

His power and love in such a way you will never be the same again, just like He did with me that day I walked into His church, heard His Word, and experienced His love, presence, forgiveness, mercy, and grace so much so I walked out a new person in Jesus Christ, filled with His Spirit and free to live for Him daily.

I wrote the opening poem within a couple weeks of giving my life to Jesus. After I got saved, I met my first Christian friend, Roger. Roger was born with handicaps, but his spirit was so alive in the Lord, he seemed larger than life. He was such an encourager and a great friend. I showed him this poem, and he was surprised I wrote it. He told me it was good, and we needed to make copies so we could drive around Nashville and post them all over the city. So, I made copies, and we drove to grocery stores and all over, hanging them around the city. Initially, I signed it anonymously because I truly wanted God to get all the glory, and I still do. Always. But I am signing my name to this poem now.

Section 1

POEMS

My first poem I wrote in 1988 was about my experience of how God moved in my heart the day I was born again.

Our Magnificent God

There was a time when my heart was lonely,
my soul was empty.
I kept searching for that great something
to fill the emptiness inside of me.
Then, one glorious day,
there was a knock at my heart.
The pounding was *so* loud,
I could not turn away, then
I opened my heart and suddenly found God.
The loneliness ended;
my empty heart was fulfilled.
God, only God, brought a blissful peace to my soul,
filling me with the Holy Spirit—
the greatest feeling I ever felt.
My soul rejoiced.
The heavens shook with victory in God!
No words could describe the magnificent joy and love
that God brought into my life.
I became a different person.
With God's strength, I am now able to turn from sin.
With faith, belief, and trust through Jesus Christ,
I can do all things through God who strengthens me.
All my burdens were lifted,
realizing Jesus Christ carried my sins
to the cross with Him.
With all those sins carried to the cross,
Jesus still gained victory over Satan.

With God's grace
and faith through Jesus Christ,
I, an unworthy sinner, received the great gift of eternal life.
I now look at life through different eyes—
through the eyes of the Holy Spirit—
looking only for the good in life
through Jesus Christ.
Seeing for the first time
the beautiful earth God made.
It is tremendous and amazing
knowing how great a God He is.
Always remember God is there for you—
through good times and
through the trials—
allowing us to be strengthened
and brought closer to God, our Father.
Always remember you have the Holy Spirit dwelling inside you
to guide you, to strengthen you.
God's love and strength are more powerful
than anything here on earth.
Stop, think, and remember: Always glorify our Father
in everything you do!

Always Faithful

For once, I was in disbelief,
Being led by evil ways.
But God showed mercy on my soul
And saved me from death and sin.
He brought life into my soul.
His light guides me.
His love protects me.
My weakness becomes His strength.
His Word shall be my every breath.
He is the Light and Truth of the earth.
I shall feed on His Word
For I will not hunger.
I shall trust in His Word
For He is always faithful.
I shall follow His light
He sent into this world
As our pure and holy example
For Christ Jesus will direct my pathway.
I shall seek His truth,
Fear His wrath,
And believe only in our true Savior,
Whom God sent to pay the debt
We could never pay
But only through Christ Jesus.

Lord, I give to Thee my whole self.
Take and do Thy will
For You know what is best for us.
You are always faithful.

For He shall inscribe His will
And His Words into my heart!

God's Gentleness

You came to me
when I was yet a sinner.
You put Your gentle arms around me;
You touched my heart
as could no other.
You opened my eyes to my sins
yet did not condemn.
You only loved me more.
You give me strength
to overcome temptations.
You comfort me in times of need.
You are with me in every breath I breathe.
When the Holy Spirit entered my soul,
I was given a new purpose in life
even though I was yet a sinner.
You have brought my dead soul to life,
giving me the desire
to live my life
as You would have me to live,
blessing me with Christ Jesus as my true example.
Although I am not perfect,
I will put You on the throne of my heart,
humbling myself to Thy righteousness for Thy name's sake.
Never will I be perfect as He.
Still, You will never turn away from me.
You are my Savior, true to Your promises.
You are my almighty God!

DONNA MCMILLIN

Unworthy Yet Loved

Jesus, my Savior,
>how unworthy I am
>of Your love and mercy.
Yet on that day,
>You saw me,
>who I really am,
>yet gave of Yourself anyway.
Oh, the suffering You endured
>carrying all our sins
>to the cross with You!
Oh, Lord,
>how sorry I am
>for the pain I caused You.
But yes, dear Lord,
>I know this was the only way
>to cleanse me pure today.
To wash me clean
>took someone holy and pure;
>it was the one and only
>Jesus, my Lord, my and your only cure.
I thank You, dear Lord,
>for paying the ultimate price
>for this world today.
If only they could all see You
>on that hill far away,
>then maybe they would realize
>You are our Savior for always.

The peace You bring to my life
      cannot be explained;
      only can it be felt and engrained
      deep into one's heart
      sent from my Savior enthroned,
      never to depart.
Your love has touched me
      and opened my heart.
Your love has given me
      peace and happiness
      that will never depart.
You have allowed me
      to experience the true love,
      one like none other,
      sent from above.
You have put trust back into my heart.
Oh, how wonderful to know
      You will always be there,
      never to forsake me
      or leave me alone anywhere.
The only faithful love,
      an everlasting love,
      always fulfilling and enriching my soul.
The empty space that once was in my heart
      has now been filled by Your love and grace.
No longer am I to be lonely.
No longer shall I be empty inside.
No longer shall I long to fill the void.
      For You have given me the greatest gift of all—
      the giving of Yourself.
The only holy sacrifice
      able to take my sins to death
      only to live again sinless and holy.
My God, how merciful and gracious Thou art
      to have loved a sinner such as I!
Thank You, our God Almighty!

$\mathcal{A}$ Prayer of Thanks

Lord,
I thank You for being my Savior, for giving Your
      precious life for me.
I thank You for Your obedience to our heavenly
      Father's will.
I thank You for humbling Yourself
      to the humiliation that day on the cross.
I thank You for being our example
      to live as You have lived.
I thank You for loving us
      enough to die on the cross.
I thank You for being so holy
      to have overcome sin and death
      and yet to rise again and live.
      Yes, the Lord lives
      and is waiting for His children
      to someday join Him.
      He took death to the grave,
      and that's where it stayed;
      yet our Lord and Savior arose.
      I thank You for Your Helper
      whom You have so graciously
      left with us to guide us,
      to be our light from within, and
      to comfort us at all times.
Thank You, Lord, for Your Helper from within, the Holy Spirit!

Gracious Father

How wonderful and gracious
    You are to us, Father.
How loving and caring
    You are to us, Lord.
You are so worthy of praise,
        every word from our mouths
        should honor Thee, oh Lord!
Thy wisdom is beyond
        our human understanding of knowledge.
Thy mercy is beyond
        our human understanding of forgiveness.
You neither forsake us
    nor hide Thy face from us.
Oh Father, how grateful
    I am for Your true
    wisdom and mercy.
You know all, and
    Your will is best
    for our lives.
How truly feeble we are
    to Thy power and strength.
Thank You, Lord, that You know all,
    and that with Your best come to us peace and rest.
Oh Father, our mere words
    cannot begin to
    give You the praise
    You deserve.
But please, Lord, take these words
    and my gratitude
    as a praise offering unto You.

When I was unwilling
    to submit to Thy will,
    You held on and
    kept me still.
You have opened my eyes
    to my sin and unwillingness to obey.
    Please forgive me, Father,
    for my disobedience and grumbling,
    and help me, Lord, to have
    the desire and strength
    to put Your will first and be willing to
    submit my way, my life to Thee, oh Lord!

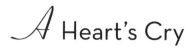

A Heart's Cry

There is this aching in my heart.
It feels like my heart is being torn apart.
The brokenness is deep;
It reminds me of my need—
My need for a Savior,
My need for cleansing,
My need for repentance,
My need for healing,
My need for You, Jesus,
To hold me up
And put me back together,
Knitted with humbleness
Knowing how fragile I am.

Places are being emptied;
I do not know where I am going.
Things pulling, and things tugging.
Lord, where am I to go?
Lord, where can I find You again?
Breathe Your life back
Into this dead life.
Breathe, oh Lord,
Before I die.
I will die without Your life.
I am lost, Lord.
Search for me, Jesus,
Like a lover searches for their lost loved one.
Search for me, oh God.

DONNA MCMILLIN

Can You find me amongst
This mess I have made?
Is there still a glimmer
Of Your life left within?
Empty me, dear God.
Father, embrace me.
Lord, how my heart aches.
You pick me up,
Dust off the ashes,
Dust off the guilt,
Clean me up,
Stand me up.

Let me see You, God,
My Deliverer,
The great almighty God.
You will restore,
You will rebuild,
You will place me, once again,
And open Your throne room
To let me see Your love,
Your wonders,
Your awesomeness.

Your Greatest Gift of All ... Love

Your love has touched me
    And opened my heart.
Your love has given me peace
    and happiness from within.
Thank You for allowing me to experience
    a true love like no other.
You have put trust back into my life;
    oh, how wonderful to know
    You'll always be there,
    never to forsake me,
    the only faithful love,
    an everlasting love.
Always fulfilling and enriching my soul.
That empty space that once was there
    has now been filled by Your love and grace.
No longer am I to be lonely.
No longer shall I be empty inside.
No longer shall I long to fill the void
For You have given me the greatest gift of all,
    the giving of Yourself,
    the only holy sacrifice
    able to take my sins to Your death
    only to rise again sinless and holy.
My God, how merciful and gracious Thou art
    to have loved a sinner such as I.
Thank You, dear heavenly Father,
    for the greatest gift of all ... Your love.

DONNA MCMILLIN

Jesus Gave His All

Oh Jesus,
>You gave it all for me—
>Your life, Your love, Yourself.

Oh, what have I given to Thee?
You paid the price
>for our every sin,
>and we think, *Oh how nice,*
>yet still we don't let You in.

You gave me joy
>that overflows,
>peace within my soul, and
>everlasting happiness!

Oh Lord, what have I given to Thee?
You do not ask for much,
>only to follow You;
>but oh, Lord, what do we do?

You give Your strength
>in my weakness,
>pick me up when I fall,
>and I don't even have to call.
>You are there!
>You never leave me!

Oh, Lord, what have we given to Thee?

Daily As We Go through Life

Daily as we go through life,
  Jesus is our guide.
He will never leave or forsake you
  but always be by your side.
Jesus is the way,
  the truth, the life.
You see there is no other way
  to rest in that great Promised Land;
  You must come to Him and obey.
God's grace is far beyond
  what our minds can comprehend.
But for us to understand,
  He promised His Holy Spirit
  He would send.
Yes, what an awesome God we serve,
  mightiest in the land,
Precious Holy Savior,
  Jesus, Son of Man.
So take hold of the truth.
The Word, it is our sword.
Jesus died on that cross,
Arose, and lives forevermore.

DONNA MCMILLIN

The One and Only True God

Thou dost amaze me
      with Your knowledge,
            knowing the desires of my heart;
      with Your love,
            fulfilling my deepest needs;
      with Your mercy,
            allowing me to experience such happiness.
Truly Thou dost amaze me;
      before I could know my own heart,
      You had given me the desires from within.
The best part about You
      is the way You express Your love,
            knowing what's best for us even when we don't,
            and keeping Your promises to us.
Thou dost have mercy upon us,
      love us,
      comfort us,
      protect us, and
      give us life.
You are truly amazing,
      The one and only true God!

Day by Day

Day by day,
        you go through life
        never knowing what to expect.
But somehow, it doesn't matter
        because we have a loving
        Father to help us along the way.
He's always there
        by our side and at times
        even holding us;
        and the sad thing is,
        we never really notice He is there.
We never acknowledge God
        or give thanks to Him
        for His many blessings
        and daily love and care.
That really bad day that comes along,
        and suddenly, you're laughing again.
Those bills that keep adding up,
        Suddenly, money unexpectedly
        comes to you.
The tears that roll down your cheeks
        then vanish as if all is well.
These are the times to acknowledge
        that God is there with you
                through all the suffering, pain, and sorrow.
                He will never leave you.
                He is always faithful in keeping His promises.
                He is the laughter that dries the tears,
                that brings joy to you after a terrible day.

DONNA MCMILLIN

And why, do you ask, does He do these things?
No, not because we love Him, but
  because He first loved us,
   that even while we were sinners,
   He first loved us.
So give God the praise and glory
   He is so deserving of.
Our God is a truly magnificent
   and loving God.
Give God a chance in your life. I did!

$\mathcal{J}$esus, His Great Sacrifice

Dear Lord,
To stop and think of the sacrifice You gave!
Oh, what an obedient and marvelous act of God!
The pain You suffered and endured
      for sinners such as I.
But then, Lord,
      oh, how glorious to know You rose again;
      what an indescribable feeling to have defeated death!
Oh Master, how I long to hear You tell
      of Your marvelous resurrection.
Oh, words could never describe
      the glory You received
      upon defeating death
      and rising to victory!
What a spectacular sight You were,
      shining bright as the Son of God,
      all in holy white.
This is the Jesus I will see
      upon my death and Your victory.
To step up into the heavens and behold
      our risen Savior in final victory.
Knowing You, You knew the victory was won,
      yet Your humbleness, even then, shows us
      exactly how great a Savior You really are,
      for us, the only one!
The only true Savior
      has won the victory.

He defeated death just for you and me!
What great a sacrifice it had to be
      to cover our sins,
      the sins of you and me! Thank You, Lord!
I know, Lord, that when I die,
      You will be there by my side.
To see the true God,
      that is where You will lead me.
Ask Him in Your precious name
      to forgive me, a sinner just the same.
To see Your light so shining
      and heaven's streets of gold,
      what a place to behold
      for those who claim
      the cross of Jesus and His holy name!

Praise His Name

Give praise to His name,
     our Savior Jesus Christ.
Honor the great name of the Lord.
Lift high our Father in heaven,
     and give praise to His name.
There is no other, no not one,
     who is so true and loving.
No one so gracious and merciful to us,
     no one but the One true God!
Thank You, dear Lord,
     for defeating death for us.
Thank You, our heavenly Father,
     for sending Your Son, our Savior,
     to die for our sins.
You truly are our heavenly Father
     for You bring us so much love
     and understanding and
     show such mercy upon us.
You are true and faithful,
     always keeping Your promises,
never leaving us nor forsaking us,
     for You are our strength.
You are always there when we need You.
You are there at those times when we
          don't see Your hand at work;
          that's when we aren't looking, and
          You are carrying us in Your arms.
You are the one and only true God!

DONNA MCMILLIN

Just a Cry from My Heart

My deepest desire
    is to live Your will,
    to live by Your Word,
    and cling to Your promises.
I long to be with You,
    seek Your glory and majesty,
    to hear Your wonderful words
    coming from Your mouth.
Hearing Your voice
    with my own ears.
What a glorious day that will be!
Lord, You know the longing in my
    heart to be with You forever,
    to be able to touch You
    and see my Savior,
    who died for me, face-to-face.
How the Holy Spirit within me
    aches to be joined with You again.
What a glorious day that will be!

I wrote this piece a couple of years post-salvation, after some heartbreaking news. Before Christ, I used to drive around with one of my young nieces and a friend of hers, living a life representative of the world. A year or two after I was saved, I found out her friend died in a car accident at only fifteen years old. I never got the chance to apologize to her for the witness I was and to tell her of Jesus Christ, the Savior of the world, who can change and transform a life from within our hearts and souls. So, brokenheartedly, I wrote this. It's very raw and maybe not anointed. I don't know. But I wanted to include it to show all the Lord was doing in me then, has done in me now, and will continue to do in me for the rest of my life here on earth. Today I advise, with every opportunity, share the love, truth, and gospel of Jesus with people He puts in our pathway every day because we never know if we will see them again or if it will be their, or our, last day on earth.

Your life changes:
 You become a new person,
 yet those who knew you before
 don't ever see your change
 because you no longer see them in person.
Then one day she dies,
 the one you didn't make the time
 to go see and tell of your new life.
She only saw you as of the world,
and now you can never share
 the love of Christ with her.
You can only pray now
 and trust God that she is with Him,
 praying that someone spoke to her.
Praying that others will look at their lives.
Stop and change their lives.
And you, you and I have got to make a difference.
You have to live for Christ
 and help others find Christ.
Don't let another one slip away.

I wrote this years ago too. I want to add that we can ask God anything. He is big enough to handle our doubts and questions; just like the man said to Jesus, "help Thou my unbelief." So do not be afraid to ask God anything, but always, always honor and revere Him.

Come to God

God is always there;
    do not fear.
Whenever you feel a burden,
    lift it up to God,
    and He will give you the answer.
God always allows things to happen for a reason.
    He wants us to be closer to Him.
Never ask, "God, why?"
    but say, "God, if it is Your will, just
    give me the strength to accept this as Your will."
God knows what is best for us;
    He allows things to happen out of deep love for us.
Who else could give their only Son
    to die for us but God and God alone!
You are never alone;
    God is always there.
Talk to God, and ask Him to help you;
    He is a merciful and loving God and full of grace.
Remember, Jesus faced suffering
    and temptation too.
Isn't it wonderful to know that our God
    knows exactly what we are going through!
Just stop and ask yourself,
    "What would Jesus do in this situation?"

An Encouraging Word in Times of Temptation

Our God is a gracious God,
        true to all His promises.
He is a loving God,
        so loving as to give
        His only Son to die for us.
We are to love our God
        with all our hearts, bodies, and souls,
        obeying His commandments,
        loving others as Jesus loves us,
        believing that by Jesus's bloodshed
        and God's great grace,
        we are given eternal life with our Lord Jesus.
Even though times get hard,
        those desires start tempting you;
        remember those desires are from Satan,
        and you are from God—
        pure and cleansed by the blood of Christ!
Yes, even if we sin,
        Jesus's blood covers our uncleanness and sins
        now and forever.
Go to God.
        He says, "ask and ye shall receive";
        confess and ask for forgiveness,
        and God will keep His promise
        of forgiving you and cleansing you of all unrighteousness,
        and spending eternity with Him!

DONNA MCMILLIN

So Thankful for My God and Savior, Jesus Christ

I love You, God.
I thank You, God.
You are always there for me
      in every minute of my life.
You have brought me from death
      into a new life with You.
You have overcome darkness for me
      and brought Your Light to shine for me.
I can look at every part of my life
      and always know You are there,
      giving me love and strength to do Your will.
You always answer my prayers,
      never leaving me,
      always listening to me and being that shoulder to lean on
      and forgiving me of my sins.
You have brought joy and peace to my heart.
You have given me a new meaning to life.
You have delivered me from darkness
      and shown me Your Light in Jesus Christ.
I know that You will never leave me
      for You are a living and faithful God forever.
You have given us grace
      through Christ Jesus our Savior.
Your love for us is too great for words.
I pray our love for You will always grow.
I want to be closer to You
      and to walk more in the footsteps of Christ Jesus.

Faith and belief in Your love, and Christ Jesus
        will deliver me from all evil.
You are truly a magnificent God!
I could never lift You as high as You should be,
        but I shall spend my life
        praising You and glorifying Your name.
Right now, I give You all the glory
        and praise You are so deserving of!

God's Miracles Every Day

God works miracles;
>   every day we see one of His miracles
>   if we would just open our eyes
>   to notice the new life we are given.
No one else but God, and God alone,
>   could make this difference in my life.
He's given me a new direction,
>   a new hope, and a new life.
My dream has become reality—
>   my dream to walk closer to God.
God has brought peace to my soul,
>   happiness to my heart,
>   fulfillment to my life.
God has given me a purpose in life;
>   that purpose is to serve God above all.
>   To give God everything I have
>   because after all, look at what

>   God gave us—eternal life!

Nothing should be too great
>   to give up for God!
We should be willing to give our lives for God's will.
Look what God gave for us—
>   Jesus Christ, His only Son, to die on the cross.
Then look at the promises God
>   gives to those who choose to follow Him.
He promises to always be with us;
>   He gave us the Holy Spirit for that promise.

His promise of eternal life
      through faith in Christ Jesus.
His promise to love us and keep us safe
      only by obeying His commands and
      living through Christ Jesus.
Now tell me,
      do we really have it so bad?
No, just remember Jesus loves you!
That is enough to get you through any day.
And look for the miracles, small and large, He blesses us with every day!

I have included so many poems about the goodness of God through salvation and the gift of eternal life because you must understand how much He changed my life the day I walked into that church and surrendered to Him. I will always be so grateful for all He has done for me!

Our God

Our God is the Holy One,
    our God Almighty!
He is a loving God;
    He gave His Son for you and me.
Our God is a giving God;
    His gift of eternal life is ours
    through the blood of Christ.
Our God is a gracious God;
    He spared us eternal death
    as Christ Jesus paid our debts.
Our God is an understanding God;
    He knows our every way,
    yet loves us still the same.
Our God is forgiving:
    "Confess and ye are forgiven."
Our God is the most high and powerful;
    through all things He is there for us,
    carrying us when we are too weak to go on,
    lifting us up when we fall,
    to be there always and forever.
    Nothing can take us from His hands.

He is a faithful God,
        keeping always to His Word
        and never breaking His promises.
        He knows us better than
        we know ourselves, yet never abandons us!
He is compassionate, caring, warm, and kind.
He is love!
He is our Savior,
        our Father, and the Holy Ghost.
He is the light, the way, and the truth.
Through Him comes all wisdom and understanding.
He knows what is best for us
        for that is His will!
He is everything to me.
He is our best friend,
        our true friend.
He is our meaning in life.
He is never demanding
        and always there to guide us.
All you have to do is
        ask, and ye shall receive.
After all, He first loved us.

I wrote this, not from a position of out-and-out sin, but from feeling like I was not spending time with God and getting into His presence. You see, when I am careless about my prayer time with Jesus, I get all out of joint. I feel like I'm dying on the inside. I so need Him in every part of my day and life. He is my life and breath!

A Prayer and Cry of My Heart

Dear Lord,
Why, oh why do I fail You so much?
Why do I push myself so far away
        from the only One who loves me so much?
Help me, O Lord, give me strength
        from Your Word to confess unto You
        all the sins against You I have
        committed and pour my soul
        out to You, dear Lord.
I've been falling far from You,
        and I'm lost without You.
Somehow, I don't seem whole
        because I'm so far from Your truth.
Help me to bow before You, Lord,
        and pour my soul out.
Have mercy on me, Lord,
        because I am so sinful.
Thy Word shall be my shield
        to guard me against all evil.
I shall turn to You for guidance,
        and You shall light my pathway.

I shall come to You for mercy,
      and Jesus shall stand before You and say,
      "Father, I paid her debt."
Oh, glory be to God, our Father and Savior, for all Your
mercy and grace to forgive a sinner such as I.

A poem I wrote for children.

$\mathcal{I}$ Love You, Lord

Listen, little children,
      to the wondrous story today.
It is of a Savior
      who loves us in every way.
He came to earth
      as yet a babe,
      growing just as you and I.
Yet, there was something special
      in the way He cried that day.
The news was heard from town to town
      of this Savior, King of all men,
      Who one day would wear the golden crown.
All were weary, but God had arranged
      that one day through this Savior,
      everyone would be changed.
He grew in His Father's likeness,
      obeying in every way,
      teaching His Father's will,
      showing us His Light each day.
All were amazed,
      some jealous, and some afraid;
      others were in awe
      because of the great miracles they saw.

Then one day
        He was betrayed
        with a kiss from the one
        who went astray.
They seized Him
        and took Him that very day
        to stand before Pilate
        to put Him away.
All were chanting,
        "Crucify Him, crucify Him,"
        but what was His crime?
        Pilate could not find,
        only He claimed the name
        Jesus, King of the Jews, they exclaimed.
They spit on Him
        and laughed at Him;
        yet not speaking any words,
        He knew this was His Father's will
        to be still.
They nailed Him to the cross,
        not knowing the loss.
Yet He looked up unto His Father
        and spoke these words of love for you:
        "Father, forgive them,
                for they know not what they do."
Yes, you, you are the one;
        look at yourself,
        the battle is won,
        He paid the price.
The greatest sacrifice of all,
        the one and only Son of God
        crucified on the cross.

He died for us;
  death was defeated
  once and for all,
  and our great gain in what seemed was lost.
But death could have no victory;
  three days later, the grave empty for all to see!
He gave His life
  so that we may live
  forever in His home above,
  seated at the right hand of God,
  filling our hearts with His great love.

A poem written like the military marching cadences.

Sound Off ... Jesus

I believe, and it's been told,
Jesus Christ is better than gold.

Eyes have seen, and it's been said,
Jesus Christ done raised the dead.

What you know, and what you've been told,
Makes the difference between hot and cold.

Open your ears and let's be smart,
Let Jesus Christ into your heart.

There He'll live and make His home
So you will never again roam.

Jump right into the river of life.
Jump right in and solve your strife.

Water to the ankles, water to the knees,
Don't be scared; jump with Me.

Rivers overflowing to the hips,
Now get ready for the trip.

Take the journey to eternal life;
Jesus is the one who paid your price.

All my years and all my days,
Jesus has always shown the way.

He will not steer you wrong;
Follow Him to be strong.

Oh, His love will never end;
With His grace, He will lend.

Look in the mirror, and what do you see?
More like Jesus I wanna be.

Sound off, Jesus.
Sound off, Jesus.
Sound off, Jesus.
Come into my heart
And be big in me.

No One But You

Lord, You are so great!
Your works are marvelous.
Your name is glorious.
Great and mighty is our God!

Your faithfulness is amazing.
Your truth everlasting.
Your love is always abundantly available.
Your goodness endures for all eternity!

Lord, we have no one else.
There is none but You.
No one to turn to.
No one who is our help but You!

No words can begin to explain
The joy that comes from You.
All I can do is proclaim
The goodness and faithfulness
Of my God, my King and friend!

How deeply my gratitude runs
Into the innermost corners of my heart,
My soul, my being
To the great I Am,
Who is my all in all,
My everything!

Praise the Lamb of God
Who reigns forever and ever victoriously!

DONNA MCMILLIN

Worthy

Oh, Lord, how I am learning
Of Your faithfulness and love.

You never stop loving us!
Not ever!

You never turn us away!
Your arms are always wide open
To receive us back in every way!

You will not say no
To the one who humbles himself
And calls on Your name,
The great name of Jesus!

In Jesus is hope forevermore.
In Jesus is sweet, sweet grace,
Undeserving yet poured out on us anyway.

Holy are You, our God.
Mighty are You!
You are so worthy,
So worthy, so worthy.
Beyond words You are so worthy!

Thank You, Lord, everlasting Father!

Shape Me

Lord, shape my heart,
      shape it in Your holiness,
      shape it in obedience.

Lord, I give You my heart
      to make it to desire You.
      Fill me with the desire for You and You alone.

Let Your consuming fire
      burn away me,
      burn away all of self.
Let Your refining fire
      transform my heart
      into Your image,
      into Your image of who I am in You.

Breathe Your breath of life into my heart.
Breathe Your desires into my life.
Shape my heart in obedience to You.

      DONNA MCMILLIN

$\mathcal{A}$rise, Church

Everywhere I turn
    I hear "Arise, church."
The Spirit of God yearns
    to lead the church in these times
    to seek the face of God.
Fire from heaven pours out
    as the Lord calls for His church.
Now is the time
    for all to come
    to Jesus as Savior and Lord.

Arise, church.
Arise, sons and daughters.
The Father desires to see His children
    return to Him in truth.
Run, faint not;
    do not grow weary
    for the Lord is our strength!

Oh Lord, how we need You!
Let Your words be in our mouths.
Let Your truth be in our hearts.

Cry for God

Oh, how the Spirit cries out in me
      to follow and yearn for You,
      but my flesh doesn't follow.

In me there will be such a cry for You, Lord,
      but then my flesh doesn't follow.
No actions come out,
      yet the cries are still inside me,
      crying out for more of You;
      yet no actions follow.

What is it Lord, what is it that keeps me here,
      here in this place of dryness,
      here in this place of barrenness,
      no submission, no obedience?

Where has my first love gone?

Lord, what is it that keeps me here
      at arm's length from You,
      in this rut?
Whatever it is,
      take it away,
      pluck it out,
      I don't want it in my life anymore!

DONNA MCMILLIN

I want to be where You are, Lord.
I want to be consumed by Your love,
abiding in Your presence
all day long!

Do what needs to be done to bring me there.
Help me to be willing to make the sacrifices
      to be obedient to the point where
        I won't let go till I know I've been with You!

The Secret Place

Lord, lead me to
the secret place in You.
Draw me near,
erase all fear.

Lord, I long to hear,
so burn all fear,
remove all dross.
I count it all but loss.

In Your presence, Lord,
is where I long to be,
with You in one accord.
Lord, set me free.

Your grace goes beyond all expectations.
Your love reaches beyond every limitation.
Your thoughts toward us are too numerous to count.
Your glory is our banner raised higher than the highest mountain.
Your hope fills our being, penetrating to our very soul and cells.
God's timing is impeccable.
It's specific, perfect, and purposeful.

God, Your love fulfills every need,
every desire, every longing.
Your love deeply feeds
my soul.

Your love is extravagant.
You will stop at nothing to display Your great love for me.
You gave up everything as You showed Your great love for the
world.

Written in June 2012 as a song.

The Place of Your Glory

Take my hand and hold it tight.
Lead me to the place
where I've not been before with You, Lord.

Lead me to that place
where I've not been before with You, Lord.

No more limits, God.
No more boxes to put You in.
No more limits.
You are the limitless God.

I just want to go to that place where I've not been before with You,
to that place where I feel Your presence like I've never felt before.

Lord, take me to the place where I've never been before.
Take me to the place where I've never been before—
        to Your glory
        to Your presence.
        (repeat 2x)

Lord, show me Your glory;
        let me see You as Moses saw You.
I want to soar to new heights.
I want to know all about You.
Release Your secrets to me, Lord.
Take me to the place where Your glory can be seen.

Lord, cover this earth with Your glory.
I want to be Your glory carrier to the ends of this earth
      so people will see, people will know
      that Your love was made known,
      and Jesus will be exalted
      and will bow down to the glory of You, Lord.

Written June 16, 2012. I felt God speaking to me to write on that morning. I pray it touches your heart and blesses you all.

Pearl of Great Price and Reward

Lord, let me hide Your Word in my heart
     and treasure like a pearl of great price and reward.

Lord, let me hide Your presence in my heart
     and treasure like a pearl of great price and reward.

Lord, let me hide Your glory in my heart
     and treasure like a pearl of great price and reward.

Keep my heart pure before You,
     and my mind set on You.

Let the motives of my heart
     be pleasing to You, Lord.

Let the words of my mouth
     magnify Your great name, O God.

You are tender and compassionate;
     Your love is far-reaching.
Your grace goes into the deepest of souls,
     into the deepest of pits,
     and rescues every hurting heart,
     every broken soul,
     and restores them
     to the place of glory
     You created them to be.

Blessed be Your name on high forever and ever, Jesus! Amen!

Cannot Be Hidden

I cannot keep Your Word, Your presence,
Your glory hidden in my heart.
Your light cannot be hidden.
Your love cannot be contained.
Pour out and overflow from my heart
to touch this world with the power of Your love and grace.

The blood of Jesus flows to the ends of the earth.
The resurrection life of Jesus awakens the darkest of souls.
Great is Your name.
Great are Your ways.
Great is Your love.

How great are You, Lord God Almighty!
You cannot be hidden forever in my heart.
How can a light be hidden?
My heart bursts to shout of Your glory,
to shout of Your love and faithfulness.
My mouth shall declare Your greatness all the days of my life.
My desire is that my life will display Your truth and love in every
step of my life.
Be glorified and lifted up, Jesus, my Savior, my Redeemer.
Let the whole world know of Your love and grace.
Let the whole world know of Your compassion
to reach Your children.
Let the whole world see the power of Your love in Jesus,
      His cross and resurrection,
      the power of life, eternal life,
      the power of love, God's great love.

DONNA MCMILLIN

How great are You, Lord!
Thank You for touching my heart.
Thank You for changing my life forever.
Thank You that I am a new creation in Christ Jesus.
Old things have passed away; behold all things become new.

Oh, Lord, how You desire that every heart cry out to You,
      and You will answer, You will deliver, You will redeem.
You will restore.
Let all mankind seek Your face.
Let all mankind seek Your forgiveness.
Let all the earth rejoice in You, O Lord God Almighty!

A song to the Lord written May 12, 2013, after my breakthrough in the airport concerning a mission trip to Haiti. (See section 3, "Testimonies and Healings" for Haiti testimony.) Sitting on the airplane, God spoke so clearly to me, and His love for me, demonstrated by the caring actions of my awesome team, overwhelmed my heart.

God's Overwhelming Goodness

Your goodness overwhelms me, Lord.
My heart explodes with thankfulness and joy.
How deep are Your words, oh Lord?
How they penetrate my heart and soul.
Deep calls to deep,
and You call to the depths of my heart and soul.
I will treasure these secret moments with You,
truly treasure them deeper and deeper in my heart.
Father, You treat me like a favored daughter,
always speaking, always revealing, always changing.
Oh, the depth of Your love.
Oh, the power of Your Word to set us free.

Father, come and dine with me.
I long to sit at Your feet.
I long to feel Your breath upon my head
        and know that I've been fed
        with the living bread.
Drinking from Your well of living waters
        overflowing from Your throne,
        knowing I'm Your daughter,
        whispering to me I am not alone.

In Your presence,
    sitting at Your table,
    soaking in Your essence
    of all that comes under the label
    of knowing You as Father
    and swimming even farther
    into the glory of Your love
    and the vision of a morning dove.

In July 2014, during a service at our church, a visiting prophet invited us to begin worshipping. I heard this song and wrote it down as the Lord spoke to me, and I finished it toward the end of her prophecy. It is just a short song, but I knew the Holy Spirit whispered these words into my heart.

God's Prophetic Whisper

Pour out Your Spirit in this place.
Words of wisdom,
Words of grace,
Words of hope,
Words of life
Enlarging time,
Enlarging space.

Bringing hope to dreams,
Sowing up all the seams,
Healing all the broken.
These are My words that I have spoken.

They will not fail.
They will not fade.
I'm the One who made the call.
I'm the One who said it all.

On April 1, 2017, I woke up in the morning with the Lord singing to me. Like an exchange, He sang to me, and I replied to Him in song. This was the first time that ever happened, and I truly needed this from the Lord! God is good!

Can You Hear Me Calling?

Can you hear Me calling?
Can you hear Me calling?

Lord, I want to hear You calling.
Lord, I want to hear You calling.

Can you hear Me calling?
Lord, I hear You calling.

I'm calling you away.
I'm calling you away.
I'm calling you away to Me.

Come to Me all who are weary.
Come to Me all who are burdened.
Come to Me all who are hurting.
I will give you rest.

Don't you hear Me calling you?
Don't you hear Me calling you?

Draw near to Me and rest.
Draw near to Me and rest.

In My presence you will find My rest.
In My presence you will find My joy.
You will find My peace.
You will find My comfort.
You will find My hope and love.

Lord, I hear You calling me.
Lord, I hear You calling me.
I will draw near to You.
I am running to Your presence.
I am falling on my knees before You.
You are my rest and strength.
You are my hope and peace.
You are my life and joy.

I run to You, my Lord.
I run to You, my Jesus.
I run into Your arms.

In Your arms I'm safe.
In Your arms I'm protected.
In Your arms I am loved!

Can you hear Him calling you?
He's calling you by name.
He's calling you by name.
Run to Him.
Run into His open arms of love!

Run to Me, My child.
Run to Me, My daughter.
Run to Me, My son.
Run into My open arms of love.

Look into His Eyes

Day in and day out,
Troubles will come,
But your strength will arise
When you look into His eyes.
And when you see Jesus,
Those troubles will fade.
Then His joy fills your soul,
And His wonder will amaze.
When you look into His eyes,
When you look into His eyes,
You'll find grace.

Nights come and nights go.
Trials linger,
But His hope shows up on time.
At the moment the Son rises
And your faith is renewed
When you look into His eyes.
And as you draw near,
You hear the heart of Jesus.
Then fear is removed
As His Spirit floods your soul.
When you see Jesus,
Those troubles begin to fade
As His joy fills your soul,
And His glory still amazes.
When you look into His heart,
When you look into His heart,
You'll see love.

So won't you run to Jesus,
Lay it all down?
That's when fear turns to hope,
Brokenness to a crown.
When you look into His eyes,
When you look into His heart,
You'll find grace.

Grace meets you where you fall.
Love knows you by your call
To pick up again,
To still call you His friend.
Love that washes you like rain.
That in you finds no shame.

Grace that pardons all your sins.
Grace that frees your heart within.
Grace that calls you His own.
Grace that never leaves you alone.

DONNA MCMILLIN

Written in September 2019, a song of the Lord. This came to me one night when my pastor and friend, apostle Michael Posey, was preaching about the wealthy place at our church.

Come to My Table

Come to My table.
Come to the wealthy place.
Freedom flows from the wealthy place.

Come to My table.
Come to the wealthy place.
Resources flow from the wealthy place.

Creativity overflows in the wealthy place.
Healing overflows in the wealthy place.
Deliverance overflows in the wealthy place.
Finances overflow in the wealthy place.

Come to the wealthy place.
Come to the wealthy place.
Overflow in the wealthy place.

Run to the wealthy place.
Run to My table.
Run to the wealthy place in Me. (repeat x 2)

I said ask and you shall receive.
Seek and you shall find.
Knock, and it will be opened to you.

Run to the wealthy place.
Run to My table.
Run to the wealthy place in Me.

An outpouring of My presence at the wealthy place,
I *am* the wealthy place.

Written November 11, 2022. I received this when my pastor was preaching about the dwelling place and heard from the Lord about changing the name of our church to The Dwelling Place.

$\mathcal{Y}$our Dwelling Place

Lord, my heart is the place You want to see;
  living there inside is where You long to be,
  dwelling, talking openly,
  knowing every part of me.

Come into my heart, Jesus,
  and make Yourself at home;
  abide in every room so no more my heart to roam.

You are my dwelling place.
  I am Your dwelling place,
  secrets to unfold
  before Your throne;
  oh, to be bold.

You are my victory
  over sin and death; I'm free.
  As You make Your home inside of me,
  renew my mind and cleanse my heart;
  oh, You have given me a new start,
  a hope restored
  from time before
  to live with You eternally,
  to hear Your voice internally,
  near to You is where I long to be,
  sitting always at Your feet.

My heart, my heart,
      the place You long to be.
My heart, my life,
      the place You long to keep.
I am Yours eternally!

I will praise You for I am fearfully and wonderfully made!

In Your dwelling place I find
Healing in Your wings,
Healing in Your breath,
Healing in Your name,
Healing in Your nature,
Healing in Your Word,
Healing in Your Son,
Healing through Your blood.

> One thing I have desired of the Lord, that will I seek: that I may dwell in the house of the Lord all the days of my life, to behold the beauty of the Lord, and to inquire of His temple. (Psalm 27:4 NKJV)

> When You said, "seek My face," my heart said to You, "Your face, Lord, I will seek." (Psalm 27:8 NKJV)

> I will praise You, for I am fearfully and wonderfully made; marvelous are Your works, and that my soul knows very well. (Psalm 139:14 NKJV)

Written November 22, 2022, during my prayer time with the Lord. It is inspired by Colossians 2:11–15.

God's Love

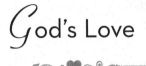

Let me tell you of a love and power like no other.
Love that reached down to the deepest pits
      and snatched us up from the grip of sin and death.

A love so strong and pure.
A love so steady and sure.

A love so powerful and so true.
A love so enduring for me and you.

A love that surrendered all.
A love that wouldn't let us fall.

A love that conquered every sin.
A love that cleansed us from within.

A love that rose in victory.
A love displayed throughout history.

A love that showed us mercy and grace.
A love that looked us in the face.

A love that sets us free.
A love that reveals who we are to be.

A love that continues to hold us up.
A love that fills to the brim of our cup.

A love that overcomes every trial.
A love that perfects His every child.

A love you will never regret.
A love that causes no fret.

A love that settles deep in your soul.
A love that makes us fully whole.

A love that reveals His heart so clear.
A love that draws His children near.

A love that meets our daily needs.
A love that provides every seed.

A love that opens His arms.
A love that dispels every alarm.

A love that gives us all power.
A love that says now is the hour.

A love that always redeems.
A love so gloriously supreme.

A love that invites you even now.
A love that waits for us to bow.

A love that declares Jesus is Lord.
A love that He offers us all He affords.

He nailed every sin against us
        to the cross of Calvary,
            defeating rulers and principalities of power, greed, and lust;
            triumphing over them publicly.

He rose on the third day;
the angels did say,
    "He is not here,
    but He is near,
    the tomb is empty."
His power revealed is mighty
    as He rose up to heaven,
    wiping away all leaven,
    seated at God's right hand,
    ready to greet us in His Promised Land.

For God so loved the world that He gave His only begotten Son, that whoever believes in Him should not perish but have everlasting life. (John 3:16 NKJV)

In this is love, not that we loved God, but that He loves us and sent His Son to be the propitiation of our sins. (1 John 4:10 NKJV)

In Him you were also circumcised with the circumcision made without hands, by putting off the body of the sins of the flesh, by the circumcision of Christ, buried with Him in baptism, in which you also were raised with Him through faith in the working of God, who raised Him from the dead. And you, being dead in your trespasses and the uncircumcision of your flesh, He has made alive together with Him, having forgiven you all trespasses, having wiped out the handwriting of requirements that was against us, which was contrary to us. And He has taken it out of the way, having nailed it to the cross. Having disarmed principalities and powers, He made a public spectacle of them, triumphing over them in it. (Colossians 2:11–15 NKJV)

Written December 2, 2022, after I saw the movie *I Heard the Bells*, the life story of Henry Wadsworth Longfellow.

Wake Up, Church

As we look at this world,
It makes our head swirl.
Where evil runs deep,
Is the church asleep?

We see the headlines
Not calling evil crime.
Wake up, oh church,
For you we search.

Is there any hope
On this slippery slope?
My soul cries out
For there is no shout.

As I look in the dark,
Do I see just a spark
Of Jesus our Light,
And ask, are we ready to fight?

If we just look with our eyes,
We only see Satan's lies.
But look beyond the veil,
No doubt Jesus will prevail.

DONNA MCMILLIN

Wake up, oh bride,
We must not hide
For Jesus, our groom,
We must now make room.

Though darkness seems to surround us,
Oh, it will not crush.
You see, the Spirit is alive.
Make ready to dive.

Dive deep in God's Word
As we take flight like a bird
And fly to new heights.
Oh God, make our hearts right.

Cleanse us anew
For You are not through.
Ready to awake,
Your church to remake.

Into Your image,
This is not a scrimmage!
God is ready to burn,
So church, make the turn.

Stand up for His truth.
Don't be aloof.
In a world that is torn,
All must be reborn.

Jesus, Savior, on You we call
For in Your presence, all must fall.
Evil is crushed,
And all will hush.
At the sound of Your roar,
Enemies fall to the floor.

Church, arise to the battle
For all will be rattled
At the sound of His trumpet.
His voice is our compass.

So do not despair.
There is change in the air,
A moving of His Spirit.
God's Word is explicit!

No room for doubt;
We must push it out.
On the truth we must stand
In this wicked land.

Hope is alive.
Revelations will strive
For understanding times
God's truth is sublime!

Our King is coming.
Listen closely to His humming
For soon will come a shaking
And a new heaven and earth awaking!

DONNA MCMILLIN

$\mathcal{A}$wesome God

Our God is an awesome God,
And with Him, nothing is impossible!

His thoughts toward us are many,
      too many to count;
      as the sands of the seashore,
      that's how often He thinks of you and me.

All that He has done,
All that He already did,
And all that He will do
He has done for us, who He loves.

No greater God could you find,
None so great and kind,
None that you can fathom in your mind,
None so great as this God of mine.

Jesus is His name,
I declare with no shame.
Oh, yes, I will forever proclaim
The wonder of His fame!

Jesus, name above all,
On His name, we all must call.
Yes, some on this Rock will fall
Because of His glory that all saw.

Make up your mind not to stumble.
On this Rock do not fumble.
For all at once will crumble
And all of us made humble.

Jesus, God's only Son,
All the glory He has won.
Through His suffering all was done
For with the Father, He made us one.

So run to Jesus, our Savior;
With Him, He shows no favor.
All can call on His name
And not be put to shame.
Coming to the river of life,
Washed clean of all strife,
And receive His eternal life.

Jesus is our only hope.
With Him, sin no more to grope.
Jesus is the only way
To the Father, so call on Him today!

ℒegacy

Lord, what legacy to leave behind
But that You, my soul did find.
Let all I do and say
Point to You, Lord, the only way!

There is no child of our own.
All we have, You have grown
Into Your great blessings in our hearts,
Knowing from You, we were never far apart.

How I wept at our loss
Until I looked upon Your cross,
Knowing there was first a cradle
For You, my Savior, born in a stable.

How my arms did ache
To hold a child in my wake,
Of a birth I would never see.
But oh, my Lord, You are my legacy!

The pain I did feel,
Lord, You knew was oh so real,
For You suffered on that tree
Just to set me free
And be my legacy.

You held me in Your arms so long
So I could be forever strong.
True love You have shown
To us and all You call Your own.

You filled my heart with those I did not birth
To show them all You gave them worth.
To help them see Your love so great
And to know You can relate
With all their pain.
Oh Lord, how it becomes our gain!

Your love began to fill every part of my broken heart,
And it was then the healing began to start.
For your promise became to me,
Better than ten sons You would ever be.
You also gave to me a loving husband.
His heart and love to me You did lend.

Lord, help me show Your love so deep,
To those who, like me, will weep.
To comfort them with Your grace,
To let them know, for them, in Your heart You made space.

You are here for all to see
You can also be their legacy.
All that matters is that You reveal
How Your great love and truth are still so real.

Even though no legacy on this earth
Through any of mine did I birth,
But the legacy I will leave,
Is in You, Lord Jesus, I do believe!
All that will far extend and exceed
All my expectancy.

Lord Jesus, You are my legacy!
Lord Jesus, You are all our legacy!

The Lord gave me this for someone who had just lost their child in a car accident.

$\mathcal{I}$n Times of Sorrow

Oh soul, oh soul, why do you cry?
My heart, my heart, let go and fly.
Jesus's arms are open wide,
There to rest and abide.

In pain and sorrow,
I will borrow
His strength and peace,
There my grief to release.

He lifts my head
Upon my bed.
Oh, my cries He does hear
As He wipes away all my tears.

My soul, my soul, how can I bear?
I know, my God, You truly care.
So release your tears, and let them flow,
And on your heart My grace and love I will bestow.

My child, I know the pain is great,
But on My hope and love take stake.
For rest assured in this time,
Knowing that you are truly Mine,
You will always find Me by your side.
And in Me, all your grief you can hide.

Oh Lord, this is more than I can bear!
My child, I know and truly care!
Rest in Me for a while.
Cast your cares upon Me, My child!
Enfold yourself in My embrace,
And I will give you all My grace.

Why are you cast down, O my soul? And why are you disquieted within me? Hope in God, for I shall yet praise Him for the help of His countenance. (Psalm 42:5 NKJV)

And he said, "While the child was alive, I fasted and wept; for I said, 'Who can tell whether the Lord will be gracious to me, that the child may live?' But now he is dead; why should I fast? Can I bring him back again? I shall go to him, but he shall not return to me." (2 Samuel 12:22–23 NKJV)

Jesus said to her, I am the resurrection and the life. He who believes in Me, though he may die, he shall live. (John 11:25 NKJV)

DONNA MCMILLIN

Give Me Your Heart

The love of God cries out to us:
      Let Me take you in My arms
      and change you into My image.
Nothing else will fill that space
      in your heart I put there
      from the beginning of time
      I created your heart for Me.
Lay down your fears, your pride.
      Run to Me; My arms are open wide.
For I will reveal and not hide
      all My love and My heart for you to abide.
For in your heart all to settle.
      My truth will not bend like metal
      but create in you great peace
      so that in Me, your fears release.
My love runs deep and red,
      on My truth you can be led;
      and with My daily bread,
      your heart and soul are truly fed.
Come drink of My living water.
      I Am your heavenly Father
      with rivers flowing within so deep,
      so My benefits and power you reap.
My heart cries out to your heart.
      I am not far apart,
      but in your heart, I will live
      if your soul and heart to Me you will give.

I Am the only one who can deliver,
so jump fully into My river,
overflowing with love and mercy,
      you will never again become thirsty.
I offer living water to your thirsty soul.
      I Am the only way to make you whole.
I Am the way, the life, the truth;
      My empty grave is your proof.
I stand at the door and knock.
      I Am the solid Rock.
All the lies My truth will unlock
      for in Me put all your stock.
I Am your living water.
I Am your hope and peace.
I Am the beginning and the end.
I Am the One you seek.
I Am the One who loves you so.
I Am the One who died for your soul.
I Am the One who rose from the grave.
I Am the One who forgives.
I Am the One who intercedes for you.
I Am the One who lives forever.
I Am the One inside of you.
I Am the One in whom you will find
Salvation, healing, and eternal life.
God and Savior, Jesus Christ is who I Am!

Jesus, My All

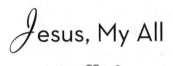

Jesus, my God, my Savior, my all,
      before You I gladly fall.
For there is no one greater;
      on this, my soul I wager.
For in You is more than enough,
      no room for worldly stuff.

For though my feet may fail,
      You will always cause me to prevail.
You anoint my head with oil;
      the plans of the enemy You did spoil.
No victory will the enemy see;
      submit to God, and he will flee.

My children arise and walk in liberty
      for in Me is your victory.
I have given you all you need;
      on My bread daily you must feed.
For in My Word is truth,
      and I am your living proof.

I will not leave you alone;
      a new name for you is written in stone.
And with My Spirit, you I will fill;
      continually in your hearts, My Word I will drill.

For under My wings you can hide,
and find shelter when with Me you abide.
For with Me nothing else matters,
and in your ears no earthly praise will flatter.
Your hope and glory are in Me;
      on worldly value you will not stew.

For on the cross I did die
      so on My wings you can fly
To heights unknown to human eye,
      into the heavens high up in the sky.

New Year 2023

In year 2023,
All this we decree:

New life, new breath,
New hope refreshed.

New season, new year,
God's voice to hear.

New faith, new doors
For even more.

New fire, new wine,
New clusters to find.

New face, new name,
His promises proclaim.

New power, new grace
In His dwelling place.

New courage to stand,
Lord, hand in hand.

Building community
Together in unity.

New boldness to declare
He will not spare.

Jesus, abundant life,
His peace above strife.

Holy Spirit within,
Bringing fresh wind.

No looking back.
We will not lack.

Running and shouting,
No room for doubting.

New alignment
For our assignment.

New truths from our King.
New songs our hearts will sing.

New enemies to defeat.
Lord, make it complete.

God, set us free
To live in liberty.

DONNA MCMILLIN

I wrote this for my nephew and new niece, Brandon and Amber, to give them on their wedding day.

arriage

Marriage is a sacred entity.
As we come together in unity,
Our homes and parents we must leave
As we lean on one another to cleave.

Two becoming one is a mystery
As we join together to make new history.
With Jesus at the very core and center,
This new life together we must enter.

Day by day, learning each other's ways,
Draw us closer, Lord, so we will not stray.
Leaning not on our own understanding
But trusting Jesus, with our hearts expanding.

For through Jesus's love, our love grows deeper.
Holy Spirit, with our hearts be the gatekeeper
To keep out all roots of bitterness.
And let our hearts flow with forgiveness.

Letting go of all hurt and anger,
So we don't put our marriage in danger
But every night as we go to bed,
Counting our blessings together instead.

Love and honor and respect—
These are the things to expect.
In our marriage with God first,
In these we will never thirst.

Love that daily grows strong
Disregards all the wrong.
As we look in each other's face,
With God's power we offer grace
To see each other through God's eyes.
We can no longer just think of I
For together we must take a stand
To always make unity a threefold strand.

Putting each other's needs above our own
For we have now become bone of bone
As we lay down our own life
And, in this way, end daily strife.

Striving to build each other up,
Pouring grace in each other's cup.
Making unity our marriage goal,
In Jesus's love we must always stroll.

Love endures and suffers long,
Not worrying who's right or wrong.
But in God, our marriage can grow strong,
Letting agape love be our heart's song.

Love covers a multitude of sin,
Then healing in our hearts begins.
God's love poured out will never fail
And will cause our love to not grow stale.

So in this life walking hand in hand,
Making unity in God our stand,
On Jesus our Rock we will build,
And our marriage will always be fulfilled.

> Though one may be overpowered by another, two can withstand him. And a threefold cord is not quickly broken. (Ecclesiastes 4:12 NKJV)

I wrote this for loved ones I see struggling so much in this world. My heart aches and at the same time rejoices because I know my God and Savior, Jesus Christ, knows their names and their hearts' cries. I desire for all to come to the knowledge of redemption, forgiveness, and salvation through faith in Jesus Christ alone! So, I leave my loved ones in the hands of the One who holds their hearts and created them for fellowship with Him!

The Father's Long-Suffering

How my soul can rejoice
And ache at the same time
Is a mystery to me.

I rejoice because You are worthy
Of so much praise and worship.
I rejoice in Your goodness
Toward all Your children
In Your tender care of those You love,
And in Your correction of those You love
In Your greatness of who You are
And in the wonder of Your love
For all mankind for all eternity.
How can we not rejoice
In our great God and Savior, Jesus Christ?
I rejoice in the outpouring of Your presence
In our hearts and lives,
Whispering Your promises to us in the night,
And proclaiming Your faithfulness to us all the day!

DONNA MCMILLIN

How I rejoice that You have
Called us by name—individually—
Knowing each of our hearts personally.
I rejoice in Your long-suffering with all mankind,
In how You desire all to be saved.

And in this my heart aches,
Knowing how much You love Your children.
How much You gave in sacrifice to us.
How much You long for Your children
To draw nearer to Your embrace and heart daily.
To know Your name and call upon You
To set the captives free,
And bring healing and salvation
To all who call upon the name of Jesus!

My heart aches as I see those You love
Trying to find peace in worldly things;
The true peace that only You can give.
Trying to find their identity by the world's definition
When You have already given them identity in Jesus, Your Son.
Trying to find freedom on their own
When You have set them free in Your truth.
And finding pleasure in what the world offers
Instead of finding the pleasure and joy
You offer in Your presence.

So I cry out to You, my God and Savior,
The One who knows their names and hearts.
I call out to You, healer and redeemer,
To mend the brokenhearted and
Redeem the lost souls.

I call out to You, deliverer and Creator,
To deliver them from bondage and
Reveal to them they were created in Your image.
You, Lord, are the One who can make whole
Through Your precious blood and great love.
So I lift every name to Your throne of grace and love.
Lord, Your will be done in every life
On earth as it is in heaven.
To You belong all power, glory, and dominion
Forever and ever. Amen!

The Lord is not slack concerning His promise, as some count slackness, but is longsuffering toward us, not willing that any should perish but that all should come to repentance. (2 Peter 3:9 NKJV)

Jesus, Our Hope

A hope that lives,
A hope that gives,
A hope that fills us all within.
A hope that says let's begin again.

A hope that is only found
In Jesus, our solid ground.
With life's twists and turns,
In our heart His hope does churn.

A hope that heals
As God begins to peel
Back all the layers,
Unveiling our betrayer.

A hope that grows
With every blow
Meant to rock
But instead unlocks.

A hope that flows
And on us bestows
A healing balm
That brings great calm.

A hope like medicine
That produces discipline,
Enlarging the space
For faith to embrace.

A hope not natural
But becomes critical
In this life we now live
Becomes our greatest motive.

Jesus's hope takes the lead.
On doubt it does not feed.
Prostrate, not with grief,
Such hope brings sweet relief.

A hope to stand upon.
True hope, not a con.
A hope that is sure;
A hope that endures.

Jesus, our true hope
In Him, our life's rope.
His hope so true
Becomes our morning dew.

Hope, amid life's demands,
Rises up and assuredly commands
All fear and doubt must surely leave.
For hope in my Savior I will truly cleave.

Hope is an invitation
For great expectation
In the working of His power
To stand like a strong tower
In the midst of all we see.
In Jesus's hope we still believe.

> This hope we have as an anchor of the soul, both sure and steadfast, and which enters the Presence behind the veil. (Hebrews 6:19 NKJV)

DONNA MCMILLIN

Now hope does not disappoint, because the love of God has been poured out in our hearts by the Holy Spirit who was given to us. (Romans 5:5 NKJV)

Now may the God of hope fill you with all joy and peace in believing, that you may abound in hope by the power of the Holy Spirit. (Romans 15:13 NKJV)

Blessed be the God and Father of our Lord Jesus Christ, who according to His abundant mercy has begotten us again to a living hope through the resurrection of Jesus Christ from the dead. (1 Peter 1:3 NKJV)

Why are you cast down, O my soul? And why are you disquieted within me? Hope in God, for I shall yet praise Him For the help of His countenance. (Psalm 42:5 NKJV)

New Life in Christ

Once I thought a little of Him and a little of me.
But of course, that was not how it was to be.
For you see, He must in our hearts fully reign.
Then the Holy Spirit can pour out His fresh rain.

Jesus makes all things become new
So that we can see with a fresh view.
Because the old things have been removed,
Jesus's blood has now made us approved.

Holy Spirit of God lives within.
Our minds and hearts He does cleanse.
He teaches us God's Word of truth,
And He is our guarantee and proof.

In Christ we are a new creation.
Between us and God, He is our liaison
So that we may boldly come to His throne
As our souls will no longer deeply moan.

Through Jesus, we have been given new life.
Like a surgeon yielding his sharp knife,
The Spirit of God begins to cut the old out.
So, our new man within rises up with a shout.

Minds are made to think new thoughts.
The Spirit of God within has fought
With the flesh of our old man
And given us God's new divine plan.

Our lives have been transformed.
Our hearts have been reformed
As we begin fresh each day
With Holy Spirit leading the way.

As He shines His bright light
On the things done in the night,
Jesus can remove the internal strife
As He gives us new resurrection life.

Jesus offers us a brand-new day,
As we learn to walk in His ways,
To make us in His glorious image
With flesh no longer the need to scrimmage.

Day by day He gives us victory
As He reveals His great mysteries.
Life will never be the same
As He writes on us our new names.

So let the Spirit of God daily lead.
With His daily bread, He will feed.
Our souls no longer will hunger and thirst
As we put our Lord and Savior first.

Therefore, if anyone is in Christ, he is a new creation; old
things have passed away; behold, all things have become new.
(2 Corinthians 5:17 NKJV)

Walking in Love

What manner of life do we walk in,
What manner of life do we lead
When we walk with our fellow man
Through this life God has given us indeed?

Do we slice and chop and cut up,
Or do we bring to the table healing balm in a cup?

Do we yield our tongue to tear down,
Or do we use our words to build a town?

Do we whisper the lies we hear in the night,
Or do we shout the words of God in the morning light?

Do we see the worst of mankind each day,
Or do we seek the best in each other and pray?

Will we let our fellow men fall to their end,
Or will we pick them up and help them to stand?

Will we hiss and point fingers at others' faults,
Or offer the same mercy Jesus deposited in our own vaults?

How can we better understand and share
The love of our God and His tender care?

Walking in unity, walking in love,
Fulfilling the Father's commands from above,
Letting forgiveness flow from our heart
With loving-kindness extended to our brother as a start.

DONNA MCMILLIN

Breathtaking

Oh, heavenly Father,
You fill us with such joy.
Your glory and majesty
Are always on display for all to see.
So breathtaking to me.

My heart exploding with such gratitude,
And I am so humbled by Your love.
Lord, I know there is nothing
You won't do for Your children.

Your goodness and blessings
Surround us constantly.
Your strength and grace
Keep us standing through all of life.

I truly cannot tell of all Your
Wonders and miracles in my life.
You have never failed me at any time,
And I know You never will.

Your faithfulness is so amazing.
Your love fills my whole being
With the greatest gift ever given
To all mankind, the gift of Jesus!

You pour out Your presence,
Inviting us in to see Your glory
And to see Your heart in even deeper ways.
Oh Lord, how can we even stand in Your presence?

Lord, You desire for us to know You deeply.
You long to have our whole hearts
To open up to You and let You in.

Oh Father, we could never deserve
All Your blessings and
The gift of Your presence
In our hearts and lives.

How You seek after us
And desire to reveal
All Your secrets to us,
And the intimacy
You offer to us.

So amazing and wonderful
Is our God and Father.
No one can compare.
No one comes close
To Your awesome love,
Power, peace, joy,
And hope You give us
Through faith in Jesus Christ!

Great are You and greatly to be praised!
Our heavenly Father, God and Savior, Jesus Christ!

The Invitation

From before the beginning of time,
Our God made a plan for an invitation.

An invitation
To know Him intimately,
To know Him deeply,
To know His Son—Jesus—
To know the secrets of His heart!

An invitation
To walk with Him,
To talk with Him,
To sit at His table,
To daily sup with Him!

An invitation
To open our hearts to Him,
To come into His presence,
To see His glory,
To touch His power,
To hear His voice daily!

An invitation
To experience abundant life in Jesus Christ,
To experience grace without deserving it,
To experience His mercy new every day,
To experience His love that endures forever!

The invitation
Jesus gives to all who come to Him
Who will humble themselves before Him,
Who acknowledge their need of a Savior,
Who understand the grace He offered,
Who believe He is the way, truth, and life,
And only way to God
Who will confess their sins to Him,
Who will repent and turn from their sins,
Who believe He died and rose again!

The invitation
To receive the gift of salvation,
To receive the gift of a new life in Jesus,
To receive the gift of a heart changed,
To receive the gift of a mind that is renewed,
To receive Jesus and eternal life
With a promise of being with
Our God forever in eternity in heaven.
To receive the gift of His Helper,
The Holy Spirit, to live in us,
To teach us all things of God,
To comfort and encourage us,
To fill us to overflowing
Where rivers of living water
Flow out of us continually!

God's heart and arms are open wide
For our invitation to join Him
In this life through faith in
Jesus Christ and experience life, and life more abundantly!

My Heart, Seek Jesus

May my heart seek Your heart.
Holy Spirit, draw me oh so near
For with my first love, I must start,
And let You hold me oh so dear.

My heart longs for You I cry.
I long to know You even more.
Fill me full; I can't run dry.
For You I worship and adore.

Lord, help me live for You alone.
Let Your rivers overflow
To depths so deep, so unknown,
Then on me Your Spirit to bestow.

Lord, there is no other love
That can come close or compare.
None below and none above.
In You there is no longer any despair

Your tender care and understanding we receive.
Your unending mercy and Your grace
Are ours when we humbly bow and believe
When we come into Your secret place.

There we find Your wisdom and Your truth,
Whispered words as we draw near.
Transformed hearts and lives are Your proof
Of Your light that makes all things clear.

You make Your home deep within us,
Giving us every part of You,
Convincing us in You we can trust.
Every aspect of Your life is true.

To You, my Savior, I surrender all
My hopes, my heart, and my dreams.
When into Your loving arms I fall,
There is mercy flowing from Your streams.

A new love I have truly found
In Jesus, my Savior and my Lord.
You have anchored my feet to the ground.
In You, my Rock, I can afford
To empty out all of me
And know in Your love I am totally free.

When You said, "Seek My face," My heart said to You, "Your face, Lord, I will seek." (Psalm 27:8 NKJV)

Every Good Gift Is from You

Lord, all we have,
All we are,
Is from You!

We give thanks to You, Lord.
You made our hands to work.
You gave us strength to live.
You make us all worthy
Through Your great sacrifice, Jesus.

You have filled us with Your goodness.
You have surrounded us with Your mercies.
You have covered us with Your grace.
You have poured Your love over us without measure.

You have taken on Yourself
All that we could not do or be,
You have poured out Your blood
All so we could be found righteous
Before our God and be redeemed.

You have defeated sin and death
All so we could have victory and eternal life.
You have given us life more abundantly
All through belief and faith in Your name.

You and You alone, Oh Lord,
Are the goodness in our lives.
You have given us the best gifts
In giving Your all to us.

You have given us everything
We need to live a life pleasing to You,
To walk in Your holiness,
To live in Your righteousness,
To move in Your authority,
To act in Your power and love,
To be the witness of Jesus Christ
To a lost and dying world.

Jesus, You are our everything.
You are our life, our being.

We give You glory and honor.
We worship You, Jesus,
As the great I Am,
As our Shepherd and Savior,
As our Deliverer and Healer,
As the Almighty God,
As the Most High God
Seated at the right hand of God,
Forever interceding for us.

Such great love we could never attain.
Such great love You freely gave.
Such great mercy on our souls.
Such great grace to love You so!

> Every good gift and every perfect gift is from above, and comes
> down from the Father of lights, with whom there is no variation
> or shadow of turning. (James 1:17 NKJV)

DONNA MCMILLIN

Holy and Mighty God

Oh, the wonders and glory of our God!
His majesty and holiness!
His grace abounds where sin abounds.
His mercy is new every morning.
His love endures forever!

Who is like our God?
There is no other, none who can come close!
Our God is a mighty God!
Our God is a fierce God!
Our God is a holy God!
Our God is righteous and just in every way!

Our God is the Lord of Hosts,
the Lord of heaven's army!
Mighty in battle is our God!
No one and nothing can stand against Him!
His name is above every name!
False gods fall before Him; they cannot stand!
Our God is on our side!
If God is for us, then who can stand against us!
There is none to compare!
Nothing can snatch us out of His hands!
Nothing can separate us from His great love!

Oh, call upon the Lord God Almighty!
He is worthy to be praised!
Call upon His name and see
    demons fall,
    strongholds broken,
    captives set free,
    the blind see,
    the deaf hear,
    the dead brought back to life,
    lives restored,
    marriages reconciled,
    hope renewed,
    new life begins.

All praise and glory to our God and Savior, Jesus Christ!
King of kings!
Lord of lords!
Wonderful
Counselor.
Almighty God,
Prince of Peace,
Restorer of the breach,
Redeemer of all mankind,
Deliverer,
Provider,
Protector,
Our shield and hiding place,
Our dwelling place,
The Alpha and Omega!
Soon coming King!

No one is holy like the Lord, For there is none besides You, Nor
is there any rock like our God. (1 Samuel 2:2 NKJV)

O Lord God of hosts, Who is mighty like You, O Lord? Your faithfulness also surrounds You. (Psalm 89:8 NKJV)

Exalt the Lord our God, and worship at His holy hill; For the Lord our God is holy. (Psalm 99:9 NKJV)

And he said: "The Lord is my rock and my fortress and my deliverer; The God of my strength, in whom I will trust; My shield and the horn of my salvation, My stronghold and my refuge; My Savior, You save me from violence. I will call upon the Lord, who is worthy to be praised; So shall I be saved from my enemies." (2 Samuel 22:2–4 NKJV)

In My Presence

There is a place I long to meet with you,
That place in your heart you long to free.
In My presence I can make all things new
And create in you what I meant for you to be.

In this place you can be free of your burdens.
In this place you can hear My heart calling,
Calling out to you to meet Me in My garden
In the quiet of the day, where all else is falling.

Come away with Me to the quiet place.
In My presence are pleasures forevermore.
In this place you leave behind the rat race.
To find My peace will be no labor or chore.

Turn from that which draws you away.
Hear my voice and come find rest.
For with Me there's no temptation to sway.
I promise to give to you only My best.

Come to Me, all you who labor and are heavy laden, and I will give you rest. (Matthew 11:28 NKJV)

Return to your rest, O my soul, For the Lord has dealt bountifully with you. (Psalm 116:7 NKJV)

One thing I have desired of the Lord, that will I seek: That I may dwell in the house of the Lord All the days of my life, To behold the beauty of the Lord, And to inquire in His temple. (Psalm 27:4 NKJV)

DONNA MCMILLIN

Just Let Go

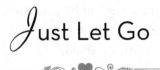

Oh, the hold of every regret,
To just let go and forget.
Grab on to life and really live,
To just let go and forgive.

Every wall comes crumbling down
As we surrender all and pick up His crown.
Lay them down at Jesus's feet,
And see our enemy flee in defeat.

Joyful life in Jesus is ours to keep,
And His peace as we lay down to sleep.
Fear has no place in our thoughts
Because through His perfect love, He has fought
Every demon and lie from the pits of hell.
Through Jesus, the enemy has been expelled.

So, look to Jesus; He is our help.
He leaves no stinging welt.
His love covers a multitude of sin
As we dive into His Word and let Him in.

Oh, Jesus desires to fill all our hearts.
Surrendering to Him as Savior is a start.
To His wide-open purposes and His plans,
Just dare look up, and take His outstretched hand,
And He will lead us to His Promised Land.
On Christ the solid Rock we all can stand.

His promise is for life more abundant here on earth.
His promises He gives for us to fully search.
There is no good thing He will withhold.
So run to His throne and be bold
To ask without any hesitation
For in Jesus there are no limitations.

Our God is greater than all.
There is nothing too big or too small
To bring to Him and believe.
For He desires to set us free
As His blood cleanses us totally.
His blood gives us all authority
To trample on our every enemy,
And put him under our feet in defeat.

To walk in His holiness is our daily call.
Filled with His Holy Spirit, we cannot fall,
Living and breathing in Jesus Christ.
Be strong and courageous, my child, now arise!

Jesus said, "The thief does not come except to steal, and to kill, and to destroy. I have come that they may have life, and that they may have it more abundantly." (John 10:10 NKJV)

Behold, I give you the authority to trample on serpents and scorpions, and over all the power of the enemy, and nothing shall by any means hurt you. (Luke 10:19 NKJV)

DONNA MCMILLIN

In You Alone, Lord

My heart, my soul, my life I give
To You alone, my Lord, to sift.

When grief and pain consume my soul,
Only You alone, my Lord, can console.

With no other, I dare compete
For in You alone, my Lord, I am complete.

To no one else I will compare.
To You alone, oh LORD, I am laid bare.

As I look to Your Word, it becomes my mirror,
And how my vision becomes oh so clearer.

To know that I am made in Your image,
With no other I need to scrimmage.

For You alone have called me by name.
I don't need to play any other petty game.

For in You alone I have my identity.
In You alone is all my entity.

For in You, my Lord, I need not strain.
For in You alone I have all to gain.

Jesus, Our Risen Lord

The scorned religious leaders took Jesus away
With the one who, with a kiss, had betrayed.
The disciples, like sheep, all went astray.
Forgotten, Jesus said it would happen this way.

Jesus, our Lord, brutally nailed to the cross,
Oh, how it became our great gain with His loss.
He willingly laid down His life; it was not taken.
If death thought it had won, it was greatly mistaken.

As He laid in the tomb of the unknown,
Hell was rejoicing; they thought Jesus disowned.
But on the third day, the stone rolled away.
No longer rejoicing, hell was put in great disarray.

As the women came to pay their respect,
It was not at all what they would expect.
An angel appeared to them to point the way
And remind them all what Jesus did say.

Then the angel proclaimed, "He is not here."
The tomb lay empty; it was very clear
That Jesus our Lord had surely risen.
Now death and the grave, no longer a prison.

All glory and honor on Jesus the Father did bestow.
From His throne, the River of Life on us freely flows.
So shout of His victory from the top of the mountains.
All who thirst come to Jesus and drink from His fountain.

DONNA MCMILLIN

Oh, lift your eyes to see our great redemption.
As Jesus arose to His holy ascension,
Our hope now found in His power and resurrection.
On Jesus, our risen Lord, is all our attention
As we eagerly await with great anticipation
On our soon coming King with glorious expectation.

> He is not here; for He is risen, as He said. Come, see the place where the Lord lay. (Matthew 28:6 NKJV)

> He is not here, but is risen! Remember how He spoke to you when He was still in Galilee, saying, "The Son of Man must be delivered into the hands of sinful men, and be crucified, and the third day rise again." (Luke 24:6–7 NKJV)

$\mathcal{A}$ Twist on Christmas

As children were brought
To the stockings now fully stuffed,
Things were not as ought.
Oh, was it found to not be enough?

Under the tree could be seen
Many gifts to be given.
All wrapped in red and green
With great bows and ribbons.

Candles in windows brightly lit,
Angels on top of the tree,
Plates with cookies already bit,
Children now running free.

Laughter could be heard
Above bells as they jingled.
But never a word
From the parents who mingled.

For though it was Christmas morn,
No manger scene with a babe on display,
Nor one look of any forlorn.
It was as just another day.

Food on the table,
Drinks all in hand.
No thought of a stable
In a far distant land.

DONNA MCMILLIN

Families all gathered, now filling the room.
Excitement and laughter from all the presents
As no trace could be found of any gloom.
Yet void of our Savior, there was a great absence.

All of a sudden, at the wink of an eye,
There was a great shaking
As bodies rose to the sky.
Would there now be an awakening?

Surely all would know
Of the prophecies long foretold
About the babe born to grow
In the Bible with pages lined of gold.

God's Word had been forgotten,
And children were never told
Of His only Son who was begotten,
And the gift they would not unfold.

Then, like from a bad dream,
I was suddenly awakened
With such a loud scream
My mind and heart were shaken.

As I arose from the bed,
My feet began to move.
In a great hurry I fled
As if only a dream I had to prove.

As I descended the stairs,
Praying as I turned on every light
To find hope and not despair,
The dream such a great fright.

As I looked all around
At the scene before my eyes,
The evidence was found
That proved nothing was awry.

The manger scene on the table,
The family Bible opened to the story
Of the Babe found in the stable,
Wrapped in all His wonder and glory.

On my knees I did fall.
My eyes filled with tears.
Then on Jesus I did call
And rejoiced when His voice I did hear.

He reminded me to declare
Of His truth and of His glory.
To my children I would share
Every detail of His cross and His story.

So, every Christmas Eve
The children gather all around
At the table where we now leave
A space for Jesus always to be found.

In our hearts He now lives
With His Holy Spirit to abide.
Abundant life God fully gives.
From His truth we no longer hide.

For unto us a Child is born, unto us a Son is given; and the
government will be upon His shoulder. And His name will be
called Wonderful, Counselor, Mighty God, Everlasting Father,
Prince of Peace. (Isaiah 9:6 NKJV)

Transparent before the Lord

Oh, to know the depths of one's heart.
To know the darkness that can hide in one's thoughts
For these we constantly wish to depart
For against these we desperately have fought.

To try to hide them even from ourselves.
To try to deny their occupancy in our souls.
From these we cannot gain any wealth.
Only to confess is to make one whole.

For from my Savior's eyes I cannot hide,
And from His heart I cannot depart.
For His arms are held open oh so wide
For me to run into, and His love to impart.

My Jesus knows every failure and success.
Yet His grace extends even to the darkest night.
A great masterpiece He painted from my mess
As He turned my darkness into His glorious light.

For every trial this life holds and does contain,
Every pit that tries to hold us in deep shame,
Every drop of Jesus's blood for us it did pertain.
On the cross, for us, He took all our blame.

With every chain His power has broken.
With every stripe His body did take.
His great sacrifice became our token,
And in our hearts His love did awake.

Oh, to know the depths of God's rich love
Poured out on me in such great overflow.
To feel His touch and see His heart from above,
What joy and peace my soul does know.

In the presence of my Savior Jesus Christ,
Seeing Him face-to-face in victory one day,
Walking into my hope and eternal life,
Never again in my life will I sway!

$\mathscr{I}$ Am My Beloved's

To try to capture the wind of the Holy Spirit
Would be like trying to capture the air in my hands.
But Jesus said to be still and wait on His gift,
And the Holy Spirit of God would be poured out on us.
And we would be endowed with power from on high.

He would be our Comforter in times of struggle.
He would be our teacher of knowing the heart of God.
He would be our helper in times of great need.
He would be our Power to overcome each temptation.
He would be the One dwelling on the inside of us forever.

He is the very breath inside my lungs.
The joy that stirs and beats in my heart.
The peace that settles deep within my soul.

His voice leads me to places unknown,
To the depths of my Father's love.
Never have I experienced so much life
Than when in the presence of my Lord.

The longing Jesus fills deep within
Cannot be attained any other way
Than to be settled in my Father's arms,
Knowing that is where my heart safely belongs.

The depths of His love, mercy, and grace
Overwhelm my heart with desire
To know His heart even greater
And search His Word for hidden treasures.

To find the greatest of gifts ever given.
To rest in my Savior's glory and presence
In the assurance of hope in His promises,
Knowing He cradles me in His embrace,
And contentment wraps around my heart like a blanket.

For Jesus has captured my heart, my soul, my very life.
Pouring out Himself like oil running over my head,
Soaking into every cell and fiber of my being.
And reassuring me I am His daughter,
And He has called me His very own.
To know that I am His, and He knows my name.

I am my beloved's, and my beloved is mine.

> I am my beloved's, and my beloved is mine. He feeds his flock among the lilies. (Song of Solomon 6:3 NKJV)

DONNA MCMILLIN

The Lord Strong and Mighty

Lord, Your Word is powerful!
As we declare Your Word,
Mountains crumble,
The enemy trembles,
And darkness flees!

Lord, You are mighty in battle.
You are a fierce warrior
Who no one can stand against.
You are our defender and protector.
Nothing shall break through Your defense.

You fight for us against our enemies.
We need not be afraid of them or anyone.
For the Lord our God goes before us,
Fights for us, and is our rear guard
Oh who can stand against our God!

The Lord is mighty in battle, strong and mighty,
And He stands for us in the midst of our enemies.
He is our shield and buckler.
Greater is the army of our God
Than those who might surround us!

We shall be like David against Goliath
Because we know the Lord is with us.
We will not be afraid of what appears as giants
For we announce we come in the name of the Lord our God.
And today, our God will cause our enemy to fall before us.

Stand up, stand up all His children
For the Lord goes before us,
And He is our rear guard.
He surrounds us on all sides,
And nothing can penetrate His wall of protection!

So take the sword of His Word,
A double-edged sword, sharper than any.
Put on your helmet of His salvation and deliverance.
Raise up your shield of faith in Him alone.
Strap on your breastplate of His righteousness.
Stand with the girdle of His truth,
And put on the sandals of the peace of His gospel.
And then stand and pray, and stand and pray again.
And watch and see the salvation of our God over the enemy
For we do not stand alone; the Lord our God Himself fights for us!

> You must not fear them, for the Lord your God Himself fights
> for you. (Deuteronomy 3:22 NKJV)

DONNA MCMILLIN

My Soul Set Free

My soul, my soul, rise from out of the ashes.
Jesus Christ has already taken those slashes.

Release the pain and the weight,
The shame that seems all too great.

You were never meant to bear it alone.
Lay it all on Jesus, our cornerstone.

Release the anger, the sorrow, and the hate.
Don't give bitterness the key to your gate.

Jesus desires to free you from those chains.
No more heaviness, causing no more strain.

Give to Jesus your life wreckage
As He turns it into His great message.

No more paths with all the twists and turns.
Into God's purpose I will finally return.

Exchanging beauty for ashes, joy for mourning,
Singing His praises to relieve all the scorning.

Through Jesus's love and grace I now live
And receive the peace and hope only He gives.

All my days now filled with His presence,
The Holy Spirit holds up in this residence.

Flowing in rivers of living waters,
Walking in confidence as His sons and daughters.

> To console those who mourn in Zion, to give them beauty
> for ashes, the oil of joy for mourning, the garment of praise
> for the spirit of heaviness; that they may be called trees of
> righteousness, the planting of the Lord, that He may be
> glorified. (Isaiah 61:3 NKJV)

The Struggle

The struggle within is definitely real
No matter how you try to conceal.
The expressions on your face
Seem quite absent of His grace.

The actions that are displayed,
Your words spoken in such haste,
All expose the struggle within,
That your emotions are in a spin.

As you allow yourself to isolate,
It's there the enemy will violate
Your heart, soul, and your thoughts
To make believe what you not ought.

Instead, it's time to now expose
The depths of the enemy's blows.
To release God's balm on the scars
And to let down all your guards.

To let Jesus's healing begin
To go even deeper within,
To cleanse out all the stain
Left behind from the pain.

Healing flows from heaven's throne.
Such great love you have never known
That touches the places once hidden,
Releasing His joy never more forbidden.
Goodbye darkness, good riddance.
No longer will you have admittance
Into my spirit, heart, mind, or my soul.
For in my Savior's love, I am made whole.

The Voices We Listen To

The voices we allow in our life
Can bring God's peace or bring strife.
The spirit behind every word spoken
Can build or cause things to be broken.

The voices we choose to listen to
Can cause rest or cause us to stew.
They can bring great confusion
And in the mind, bring great intrusion.

The voices we choose to give room
Can cause God's truth to bloom
And bring to the heart conviction,
And with that, beautiful transformation.

Don't allow in just any voice.
We really do have the choice.
To choose death or life, we decide
For in God's Word, we need to abide.

The enemy will try to convince us
With words that seem to be true.
But they will squeeze in and shut every door,
And cause us to crumble to the floor.

Trust in God's Holy Word instead
For His truth is our lifelong thread
That brings such peace to our soul
And makes us completely whole.

So shut every other voice down
Before it causes us to drown.
Only the voice of God will bring peace,
Sweet rest in our soul to release.

Do not despair; the Lord hears our cries.
His truth will diminish all the devil's lies.

Holy Spirit, come and rest upon us,
And in Your presence, we will trust.
Holy Spirit, reside within us,
And silence the voices that try to demand,
The voices that try to confuse,
The voices that try to destroy.
These are all the tactics of the enemy.
But Oh Lord God, we trust in You
That You have and continue to destroy
Every lie of the enemy coming against us.
You tear him down and crush him under our feet.
And give us sweet victory in the powerful name of Jesus.
And in His victory over death, sin, and the grave,
We rest in Your everlasting arms of faithfulness
Knowing You will never allow Your children to be defeated.
You give us power dwelling within us to overcome
All the attacks of the enemy each and every day.
Holy Spirit, dwell within us, overflowing with Your power and
Presence, and bring peace to our hearts, souls, and minds,
Once and for all, knowing Your goodness and power
And that all things are under Your feet permanently.

Captivity Captive

Oh, how quickly distractions enter in
To capture the heart and attention,
To turn our devotion away,
And cause our walk to stray
From the One who gives us life
To keep our focus on the strife.

Keep watch over our thoughts
For this Jesus has greatly fought
To give us power and authority
To overcome attacks from the enemy,
Who targets our minds to cause instability.
But abide in God's truth and be set free.

Keep our eyes fixed on the author and finisher of our faith,
On Jesus Christ the One in which our soul is truly bathed.
Do not look to the left or to the right
But straight ahead on His glorious light

Taking every thought captive is a daily battle.
Our weapon is not carnal to cause us to rattle,
But mighty in God to pull down strongholds.
So by His power, stand courageous and be bold.

> For though we walk in the flesh, we do not war according to the flesh. For the weapons of our warfare are not carnal but mighty in God for pulling down strongholds, casting down arguments and every high thing that exalts itself against the knowledge of God, bringing every thought into captivity to the obedience of Christ. (2 Corinthians 10:3–5 NKJV)

> Therefore He says: "When He ascended on high, He led captivity captive, and gave gifts to men." (Ephesians 4:8 NKJV)

Jesus, the Answer We Carry

We carry the answer in us.
The answer for the lost,
The answer for the broken,
The answer for the battered,
The answer for the lonely,
The answer for the captive.

How will they know
Unless we go?
How will they seek
Unless we speak?
How will they know
Unless we show?
How will they know
Unless we go?

Religion is the trap.
Drugs will cause you to snap.
Sex will take your soul
And make you go low.
Power does not bring peace.
Greed does not bring increase.

Let me tell you, my friend,
And this I will show.
The answer is not a trend
But the precious blood that flows
From the cross that makes us whole
To the empty grave, that now cannot steal.
To the resurrection that proves He is real.
For Jesus, the only Son of God,
The sandals of peace He did shod
To take away our sins
For all to truly win.
Jesus is the answer to every question and need.
His death and life have truly set us all free.

The Wonders of Our Great God

I will sing of Your glory.
I will sing of Your praise.
I will sing of Your wonders,
And sing of all Your ways.

Your wonders never cease to amaze.
Your love pours out like rain over us.
Your grace flows like deep rivers.
Your mercy like balm to a weary soul.

Your salvation through Jesus, a free and perfect gift.
Your peace weaves through our hearts and minds.
Your comfort a warm and gentle kiss and embrace.
Your nearness a welcoming presence day and night.

Your power overtakes the greatest obstacles.
By Your strength we can leap over walls.
Your goodness expands in every area of life.
Your holiness shines in the darkest night.
Your righteousness like the rising of the sun.

Your life and blood poured out as a holy offering.
Your burial and resurrection were no mistake.
Your victory over the grave does loudly declare.
Your name breaks every bond and chain.

DONNA MCMILLIN

Your hope abounds in every lost heart.
Your joy bursts through all pain and brokenness.
Your truth reigns in every wayward thought.
Your faithfulness steadies like the beam
Of a lighthouse in a great storm.

No one compares to our God and Savior Jesus Christ.
No other name by which we may be saved.
Our Creator and healer who formed us in our mothers' wombs.
The One who knows our names calls us now to come out of the
Darkness and into His glorious light.
Our King forever who draws us closer to Him,
To know Him more intimately day by day.
Holy Spirit, who lives in us to empower us to walk in all His ways,
Our soon coming Redeemer who will reign for all eternity, invites
Us to live eternally by His side.

The Goodness of Our God

The goodness of our God is beyond comprehension.
His love follows us day by day into the night.
Yes, beyond what we could ever imagine or think,
Our amazing God touches our lives every day.

Like a father, our heavenly Father treats us as His children.
He draws us so near and whispers in our ears.

And if there is any discipline to be had,
He lovingly, but firmly, corrects us.

Even in the midst of sufferings and trials,
You can hear Him whispering in our ears,
"Peace be still, My dear child,
And in My presence come and rest."

If we keep our eyes on Jesus
Through every storm and trial,
We can still have joy and rejoice in His faithfulness.
There is nothing that He does not know or see.
His infinite wisdom knows no lack.

God Made Flesh

Jesus:
God became man to save all of His creation.
Fully God, fully man—God's mysterious revelation
Jesus, God's glorious redemption plan.
In Him we wholly trust, not in any man.

Jesus was God's exact image.
Jesus's life reveals God's lineage.
On Him all of God's glory rested.
All of Jesus's life He was tested.

By those who would never believe,
And by the one who tries to deceive,
Jesus through every test did reveal
On Him, God did forever put His seal.

Jesus is the King of kings.
Out of Him flow living springs.
And the only Lord of lords.
In Him are everlasting rewards.

We dare not trust in worthless idols
For Jesus, our Savior, has no rivals.
He reigns in heaven on His throne.
In Jesus, God was made fully known.

He is the image of the invisible God, the firstborn over all
creation. For by Him all things were created that are in heaven
and that are on earth, visible and invisible, whether thrones or

dominions or principalities or powers. All things were created through Him and for Him. And He is before all things, and in Him all things consist. (Colossians 1:15–17 NKJV)

For in Him dwells all the fullness of the Godhead bodily. (Colossians 2:9 NKJV)

To know the love of Christ which passes knowledge; that you may be filled with all the fullness of God. (Ephesians 3:19 NKJV)

What We Leave Behind

One day here, we never know.
In the next, what shall it hold?

To live our lives fully to the end,
And with God's truth, never to bend.

What will we do?
What will we say?
What will be due?
Where will we stay?

How do we live?
How do we give?
Walking alone in the dark,
Letting God's light be the spark.

What will we leave behind?
What will our children find?
Will it all turn into rubble,
Or cause the young to stumble?

How can we live our lives to the full?
How can we know the heart's greatest pull?
Live for Jesus, who made it all possible.
Abide in Him to make your life remarkable.

Blessing of Children

Children are a blessing, the Bible reads.
Each started their journey with a seed.
From a husband and wife in sweet love,
A love given by our Father from above.

A life that grows inside the womb,
Nine months for this baby to fully bloom.
Gaining nutrients to live and survive,
Through the birth canal and come out alive.

Pains that have no match at each birth,
But as babe is held, we know it was worth.
This child, such a great wonder and mystery
Of God's great creation in all of history.

And with each dainty breath the babe takes,
Know that you will surely make mistakes.
But with each new day comes a fresh start
To step into the role God did you impart
And know the impact on your babe's heart.

Behold, children are a heritage from the Lord, the fruit of the womb is a reward. (Psalm 127:3 NKJV)

The righteous man walks in his integrity; his children are blessed after him. (Proverbs 20:7 NKJV)

All your children shall be taught by the Lord, and great shall be the peace of your children. (Isaiah 54:13 NKJV)

DONNA MCMILLIN

Come, you children, listen to me; I will teach you the fear of the Lord. (Psalm 34:11 NKJV)

Therefore you shall lay up these words of Mine in your heart and in your soul, and bind them as a sign on your hand, and they shall be as frontlets between your eyes. You shall teach them to your children, speaking of them when you sit in your house, when you walk by the way, when you lie down, and when you rise up. And you shall write them on the doorposts of your house and on your gates, that your days and the days of your children may be multiplied in the land of which the Lord swore to your fathers to give them, like the days of the heavens above the earth. (Deuteronomy 11:18–21 NKJV)

No Condemnation

Guilt and regret tear us up inside,
The enemy's tools used in disguise.
For in Christ there is no condemnation.
Grace He offers without hesitation.

Boldly Jesus says we can come to His throne.
Left to our own escapes only deep groans.
Do not try to carry them; lay them down at His feet.
His love, mercy, and forgiveness there we will meet.

Oh, dear Lord, how badly we daily tend to fall.
But for the righteous, You pick us up as we call.
You do not forget us or leave us all on our own.
Through faith in Jesus, the way You have shown.

So, dear children, gather around with ears to hear.
In Jesus, our Savior, the way is made clear.
So surrender your fears and your hearts of stone,
And I will replace in your heart one of My own.

Holy Spirit, our teacher and our very breath,
As we surrender to Him, we find true rest.
He promises to fill us with rivers of living water.
His Spirit to refresh and become our life pump starter.

> Therefore there is now no condemnation [no guilty verdict, no
> punishment, no adjudging guilty of wrong] for those who are in
> Christ Jesus [who believe in Him as personal Lord and Savior],
> who live [and] walk not after the dictates of the flesh, but after
> the dictates of the Spirit [John 3:18]. (Romans 8:1 AMP, AMPC)

DONNA MCMILLIN

Stir Yourself Up in Our Mighty God

Lately, when I find myself having to fight off discouragement
And keep the shadows from blocking God's light,
I remind my soul to hope in the Lord.
To stir myself up in the Lord,
In His amazing faithfulness,
In His never-ending love,
In His abundant grace,
In His unfailing truth.

Awaken my soul.
Open my eyes.
See the goodness of our God.
He never fails us or forsakes us.
He is always with us, leading us.

Lord, I'm reminded of how You always come through for me.
I'm reminded of the nights I know You were with me.
I'm reminded of Your promises You whispered in my heart.
I'm reminded of how truly great You are.
I'm reminded of Your tender care of my heart and soul.
I'm reminded of Your peace You bring in the midst of chaos.
I'm reminded of who You are, our great and awesome God.
You spoke, and it was.
You commanded, and it stood in place.
You breathed and formed creation out of nothing.
You brought the light of the world to shine in the darkness.

And so, I remember who You are
And know You are enough
To speak Your peace to my soul,
To bring Your hope amid all doubt,
To pour out Your love to renew my heart,
And to stir me once again.
To look up and know You are near
And see where my help comes from.
To look upon the wonders of Your glory and power
And to know I am Yours.
And to know You are mine,
Forever and always.

So stand up, oh my soul, and do not hide.
For the Lord, strong and mighty, is on your side.

Life's Ups and Downs

All the many ups and the downs,
All the times I've had to turn around,
Through all the back and forth,
I can say He made it all worth.
In all the trials and the tests,
He is always at His best
To stand beside me all the way,
And help me make it through another day.

So many times I am reminded in the darkest of days,
My Savior is walking with me and showing me His way.
He guides me with His words of truth
To lovingly keep from going aloof.

Oh, how my heavenly Father shows His love to me
And makes me to grow like a tree with roots down deep.
He pursues me in the day and into the dark of the night
To break through the darkness and shine His great light.
Oh, how I see my deep need of Your cleansing blood.
Oh, Holy Spirit, come and wash me clean like a flood.

I stand in awe of Your glorious presence,
The place where I find my soul's deliverance.
So walk with me, Lord, in these coming years,
And put to rest all the doubts and the fears,
Knowing my help comes from the Lord
And standing on Your Word as my sword!

Death is not the end by far.
The grave no longer holds us in.
Our heavenly home above the stars
Is by far the greatest win.
Jesus Christ died on the cross.
Laid in the tomb, not all was lost.
Rose forever up from the grave
To gain our freedom and be saved.
With His promise to return,
The enemy forever will burn.
To live in our heavenly mansion,
Jesus is now making expansion
For us to join Him in the air,
Knowing soon, we will be there.

DONNA MCMILLIN

Who Is Like Our God?

Who is like our God?
The Lord, strong and mighty,
The Lord mighty in battle.
The Lord of Hosts is His name.
The Lord of Hosts of heaven's army.
The multitude of heaven's army He captains,
And none can come against such a force!
All of hell trembles at the sight
Of Jesus, arrayed in His warrior battle attire,
Seated on His horse with all of heaven's army behind.

Who can stand against our God?
None on earth or in heaven or below.
None can compare or come close to His glory and power
For His righteousness and holiness overpowers,
And all of hell cannot overthrow.

God's power is a force not to be reckoned with.
None can stand in His glorious presence.
Behold the Lord who stands in victory.
Behold the Lord who holds all keys in His hand.
Behold the Lord who comes like lightning.
Behold the Lord who thunders from heaven.
Look up and behold the Lion of Judah
Who comes to reign forevermore.

During our preservice prayer and worship service on Sunday, October 1, 2023, at The Dwelling Place, the Lord opened the curtains of heaven, and we saw what worship in heaven looks like. It was powerful and has changed our services.

In the Presence of Our God

As prayer was lifted up,
Precious oil filled each cup.
Calling out His mighty name,
Our hearts will never be the same.

The sound of heaven rushing in
As the worship soon began,
Angels spread out everywhere.
Shouts of praises in the air.

All at once began to dance.
A glimpse of heaven we did glance.
The people's voices rising up,
Today with Jesus we did sup.

As I began to look all around,
What I saw was so profound.
Smiles on faces becoming bright
With God's great majestic light.

What a wonderful, glorious scene
From heaven could now be seen.
Of His glory our hearts did sing
To His presence we did cling!

$\mathcal{A}$n Awakening

Open the door, and remove the veil.
Will it be heaven, or will it be hell?
If you choose Jesus, then you prevail.
If not, the enemy has put you on a derail.

I've got to be honest, cuz it's time to get real.
Jesus gives eternal life; the enemy wants to kill.
His deception is great, and it goes deep,
Wanting to put us all into a spiritual sleep.

Jesus said He is the truth, the life, and the only way.
Any other path to the Father will lead you astray.
You see, you have to understand God's great love,
Sending Jesus, the only pure sacrifice, white as a dove.

For all have sinned and fallen short of God's glory.
Jesus laid down His life to replace our story.
The story of a life destined for eternal death,
But Jesus's resurrection brought life and gave us breath.

The blood Jesus shed on the cross for you and me
Is the only way to be cleansed and made free.
No other can claim this passage of right
Jesus proved for us; He was willing to fight.

You may think you're right in your own eyes,
But Satan is filling you with his lies.
This may sound hard but not trying to be harsh.
God's Word is the truth; this is no farce.

Jesus forgives, saves, heals, and delivers.
Oh, His love is like a never-ending river.
In Jesus Christ, I am now found
As a daughter of God, no longer bound.

God has given each of us the choice.
He will not silence anyone's voice.
But know that our decision decides the place,
Whether we choose His forgiveness and grace
Or if we neglect so great a love displayed.
Let God's truth and love help persuade
To choose to repent of Satan's great charade
And begin to see our Savior arrayed
In all His splendor and majesty portrayed.
And in His love, we will never be dismayed.

Believe in our hearts and confess with our mouths
Jesus Christ, raised from the dead with great shouts,
Jesus, God's only begotten Son, died for us to be saved.
His blood shed for us to be delivered from the grave.

One day, when we take that last breath,
We will all have to face our individual death.
Will you choose Jesus who offers life, abundant life now and
Eternal life,
Or will you reject the Savior who loves you greatly and trample on
His gift
Of forgiveness, grace, love, healing, and salvation,
Letting the enemy steal what God meant for you,
And spend eternity separated from God forever?

There is so much more than just
Knowing Jesus as your Savior,
Completely walking in His truth, power, and favor,
To have a life totally surrendered,
Not just be a Sunday church attender.
So lay your life down at the foot of the cross,
And never look back at all that is now seen as dross.
For in Jesus, we have more than we need.
Let His Word be our compass, and give Him the lead.

$\mathcal{A}$ Shadow

Look behind you; there is a shadow who follows you.
It is your child, niece, or nephew who looks up to you
without your knowledge.
This shadow imitates everything that you do or say.
They see the real you behind the mask.
Daily they are watching you to see the man or woman you are.
Will they see the man or woman God made you to be?
You are an example God has put before them
to show His love and power to
reveal His grace and mercy to
and to lead them to Jesus personally.
They are your shadow and copy all you do.
They feel the brokenness of disappointment and
understand the frailty of mankind in you.
But can you teach them through your mistakes
about the mercy, grace, and forgiveness
of the One and only true God
and humbly lead them to the cross
and His place of repentance and cleansing?
Will you see the shadow God has put in your life
and choose to be the light of a Savior
who loves them despite their failures?
Can you show them
there is victory with every fall that you make?
And show them God
will never fail them
and is right there to give them grace.

Ready to pour out His love when they humbly fall
before Him and confess their sins to
the One who paid it all for them?
Your shadow is following you.
Look around and see
who is standing next to you,
and see if you can take their hand
and lead them to God's great commands
and way and truth.
Let them know He is always
waiting there for them
with open arms
to receive them
when they humble themselves,
repent, and turn to Him.
To give their hearts
to their God and Creator
who truly loves them
and gave His all for them.
So understand if they are around you,
God has given you all the grace you need
to guide them into the purposes and plans
God has created them to be.
God will guide your every step.
Rest assured He is by your side
in every situation you will face.
So turn your eyes to Jesus
and His Word for guidance,
and let His Holy Spirit
be your guide to lead
the shadow that follows you.

So do not fear to take responsibility
to step out in faith,
and begin to teach
them God's Word of power
and of truth that will set them free
and give them purpose and identity.

Train up a child in the way he should go, and when he is old
he will not depart from it. (Proverbs 22:6 NKJV)

Therefore you shall lay up these words of mine in your heart
and in your soul, and bind them as a sign on your hand, and
they shall be as frontlets between your eyes. You shall teach
them to your children, speaking of them when you sit in your
house, when you walk by the way, when you lie down, and
when you rise up. And you shall write them on the doorposts
of your house and on your gates, that your days and the days of
your children may be multiplied in the land of which the Lord
swore to your fathers to give them, like the days of the heavens
above the earth. (Deuteronomy 11:18–21 NKJV)

DONNA MCMILLIN

Thoughts after hearing about a death in the family. God is the keeper of life and knows every line and order of all our lives and time in general. He puts the pieces together and holds us all together in Him!

God, the Keeper of Time

Life is a puzzle.
Piece by piece,
All held in God's hand.

God sees the big picture.
He knows every line.
He places each fixture
In His order of time.

Piece by piece,
Layer by layer,
Line by line,
He is the keeper of life.

In His hand He tenderly holds
Each piece of all His creation
So that at all times, we behold
In us, His beautiful transformation.

Piece by piece,
Layer by layer,
Line by line,
He is the keeper of creation.

As He lays each piece down
In His perfect time and order,
There appears to be a crown
Reaching from border to border.

Piece by piece,
Layer by layer,
Line by line,
He is the keeper of time.

God is the puzzle maker.
In Him we can fully trust.
He is our bondage breaker.
Hope in Him; He is just!

The Maker of Heaven and Earth

Lord, when I look up into the expanse of the heavens,
> You are greater!
When I look at the depths of the oceans,
> You are deeper!
When I look at the height and glory of the mountains,
> You are higher and more glorious!
You created all that is on the earth, above and below;
> You are the great I Am!
And Lord, looking at all You have created,
> I know there is nothing too hard for You;
> There is nothing You cannot do!
You are marvelous in all Your ways,
> More powerful than anything or anyone.
Just calling out Your name, Jesus,
> Causes demons to flee, and the earth to tremble.
Mighty is our God;
> There is none like You.
> Our hope and trust are in You, O God.
The Maker of heaven and earth,
> The One who breathes and gives life,
> And the One who controls it all!
We look to You as our help
> And our strength and shelter;
> You are our protector and our shield.
> You are our portion forever,
> And in You is great joy and peace forevermore!

Through Struggling Times

Dear God, are You still near
As I hold on oh so dear
To find Your great strength,
Oh Lord, at any such length?

My heart cries out,
My cries like shouts.
Thunder on the inside
I can't begin to hide.

My heart seems to crumble.
Oh Lord, don't let me stumble.
In the dark of the night,
Oh Lord, shine Your light.

To help me find my way
Out of the darkness into the day,
Up out of this pit so deep,
Awaken me out of this sleep.

In my heart, there seems to be a great crack.
Oh Lord, is there a way to get back,
Back to the peace once lodged in my soul,
To the place where Your love again makes me whole?

DONNA MCMILLIN

Holy Spirit, reach deep down into my being.
No longer from Your presence am I fleeing.
So hold me tight in Your loving arms
For I know in You is my help, not harm.

As the dawn begins to break,
My enemies tremble and shake.
For therein lies the mystery,
My Jesus, my sweet victory.

Hope in the Loss of a Child

My heart cries out in pain.
On my soul, so much strain.

The joy and life of my child,
My thoughts, how they run wild.

To one day look and life is gone.
Oh, where is my heartfelt song?

My life will never be quite the same.
All these emotions, Your help to tame.

My child, my life, how can it be?
Oh Lord, that is so much to ask of me.

But then I find myself on my knees
And remember, Lord, this happened to Thee.

You gave up Your Son to set mine free
To be forgiven, cleansed, forever in eternity.

On this, Your promise, I can stand
That my child is now in Your hand.

And when my breath draws to an end,
I know my child I will see again.

In this time in between,
On You, help me to lean.

DONNA MCMILLIN

To trust in Your unfailing love
Given daily from Your heart above.

Through the struggles, Lord, You are near,
And my nightly cries, You will surely hear.

To carry me through each day to live,
All Your strength to me You daily give.

So, as I kneel once again,
You stick closer than a friend.

Lend me Your arms in which to hold
My life, my heart, so it never grows cold.

To always run boldly to Your throne
And know Jesus is my cornerstone.

And in Your love is my abiding hope,
In this truth I cling to as my life rope.
To once again see my sweet child,
Through Jesus we will be reconciled.

Anchor of My Soul

On Jesus Christ my hope is built,
And in Him is the anchor of my soul.
Through life struggles I will not wilt
Because in Jesus's sacrifice I take hold:

Of His strength to uphold me each day,
To keep me near Him, to not go astray.

Of His shelter as my refuge,
In His safety from great deluge.

Of His love that engulfs my being,
So life-giving and so freeing.

Of His truth that has set me free
And goes deep like roots of a tree.

Of His peace that fills my heart and mind;
Such peace, in nothing else will I find.

Of His goodness that He pours out
I cannot but proclaim and shout.

Of His compassion that seeps like rain
In my soul to remove life's great pain.

DONNA MCMILLIN

Of His faithfulness He does not withhold
From this faithless one, in Him I take hold.

Of His sacrifice and His blood
That cleanses my soul like a flood.

Of His life and glory I behold,
Jesus is the anchor of my soul.

Through all life's struggles and strongholds,
Oh, Jesus, be the anchor of my soul!

Wait on the Lord

Wait on the Lord, oh my soul,
For His mercy is new every morning.

Wait on the Lord, oh my soul,
For His love endures forever.

Wait on the Lord, oh my soul,
For His compassion fails not.

Oh, wait on the Lord.
He is from everlasting to everlasting.

Yes, wait on the Lord.
His faithfulness knows no end.

Wait on the Lord, oh earth,
And see His justice will prevail.

Wait on the Lord, oh nations,
For from His throne His righteousness rules on high.

Wait on the Lord, oh kings,
For He reigns as King forever.

Oh, my soul, wait I say on the Lord
For He comes like thunder to receive His children.

Wait on the Lord; be of good courage, and He shall strengthen
Your heart; wait, I say, on the Lord (Psalm 27:14).

But those who wait on the Lord shall renew their strength; they Shall mount up with wings like eagles, they shall run and not be weary, they shall walk and not faint (Isaiah 40:31).

Wait on the Lord, and keep His way, and he shall exalt you to Inherit the land; when the wicked are cut off, you shall see it (Psalm 37:34).

I wait for the Lord, my soul waits, and in His Word do I hope (Psalm 130:5).

The Lord is good to those who wait for Him, to the soul who Seeks Him (Lamentations 3:25).

This Christmas Babe

Such a precious Babe that was born
For a world that was in so much forlorn.

In the lowly stable manger was laid
The Son of God, the price to be paid.

God's plan for mankind set in place,
Our humanity and sin we must face.

The birth of the Savior, the angels announced,
Our ways of sin now must all be renounced.

The shepherds and wise men traveled from afar
To see His glory shining greater than any star.

All creation looked on the Babe in such great wonder.
His future foretold, sin and death forever put asunder.

For in the birth of this holy blessed Child came forth
Salvation, peace, and hope, with Jesus the Source.
As all of heaven then surely proclaimed,
Mankind and earth have been reclaimed.

So in this season, Jesus's birth we celebrate,
God's great love forever to demonstrate,
Causing all the world to see and meditate
On the great eternal hope His birth did create.

For unto us a Child is born, unto us a Son is given; and the government will be upon His shoulder. And His name will be Called Wonderful, Counselor, Mighty God, Everlasting Father, Prince of Peace. (Isaiah 9:6)

"Behold, the virgin shall be with child, and bear a Son, and they shall call His name Immanuel," which is translated, "God with Us." (Matthew 1:23)

Section 2

DEVOTIONS, THOUGHTS, AND PRAYERS

WAY OF ESCAPE

$\mathcal{I}$n July 2014, in the morning as I was beginning to pray, the Lord put a picture and a thought in my head. I envisioned someone in a room and watched as they began looking for a way out of that room.

Most places or rooms will have emergency evacuation routes posted, notable exit signs, or at least a doorway to exit (or even enter). Therefore, in the event of a bad circumstance (storm, shooting, or some other kind of crisis), you would follow the plan of emergency evacuation to carefully lead you to the closest route to safety.

As Christians, we sometimes find ourselves in a situation or room that begins to look like disaster or danger is about to happen. We will look for a way of escape or way to get to safety. So, what are we searching for? For me, because of the lessons demonstrated through the years, I definitely look for the emergency exit signs. I laugh because when my husband and I go to the movies, the theater will put a screen up that says be sure to identify the emergency exit signs/doors in case of an emergency. And yes, my eyes immediately locate them.

The Lord also teaches us how to look to Him to get out of situations. First Corinthians 10:13 says, "No temptation has overtaken you except such as is common to man; but God is faithful, who will not allow you to be tempted beyond what you are able, but with the temptation will also *make the way of escape*, that you may be able to bear it" (emphasis added). You see that? God is faithful, and He will make a way of escape in times of temptation, or any situation.

So when we find ourselves in a situation, temptation, trial, tribulation, or danger, we need to seek God first and submit the situation to Him.

Hebrews 12:2 says, "Looking unto Jesus."

Colossians 3:2 says, "Set your mind on things above."

Matthew 6:33 says, "But seek first the kingdom of God."

James 4:7–8 says, "Therefore submit to God. Resist the devil and he will flee from you. Draw near to God and He will draw near to you."

First Chronicles 16:11 and Psalm 105:4 say, "Seek the Lord and His strength; Seek His face evermore!"

Psalm 119:45 says, "I will walk at liberty, for I seek Your precepts."

Psalm 27:8 says, "Seek My face."

Throughout scripture, God reminds us to look up and seek Him when we find ourselves in any situation. Seek the Lord where He is. He is always there. He never leaves us or forsakes us. He says He is with us always, so somewhere in our circumstances, God is in the midst. We must fix our eyes on Jesus, the author and finisher of our faith, and seek the way of escape God has made for us.

The Word of God also narrates the lives of past saints and sinners as examples of how we ought to live and what we should do. First Corinthians 10 includes several noteworthy accounts. Look at scriptures to see God's truth and to find guidance for how you need to act or respond in the situation. Somewhere, God has already made a way of escape; you just have to look for it. Ask, seek, knock. God will show you the way. Jesus said, "I am the way, the truth, and the life." Seek godly counsel. If I need medical attention, I am not going to go to a financial person or vice versa. Likewise, I know in any situation, my help comes from the Lord, the Maker of heaven and earth.

- Know you are not alone. First Corinthians 10:13 reminds us that our experiences are not uncommon to mankind. Others have gone through what you are going through. Seek those who have found healing through it and talk to them, not those who are still angry or bound.

- Look up scriptures that relate to your situation. God's Word is alive and is life to all who hear and listen. God's Word breathes new life into our perspectives. It helps us to see where we are, where we need to be, and where we need to adjust. Things are not always the way we see them. Our cells of recognition can alter our viewpoints, but when we look in God's Word, we can combat lies and half-truths with the complete truth. We only see in part, but God sees in whole, the big picture.

- Submit to God. Submit your desires and thoughts to Him. Ask Him to search you and see if there is any sin or wicked thing in you.

DONNA MCMILLIN

- Next, you need to repent if God reveals any sin in your life or heart. If you have gotten yourself into a situation through your own choices, confess it to God and ask forgiveness. This is a first step to freedom, to seeing God, and to seeing clearly. Maybe you should not even be in this place, and God has repeatedly warned you against going, but you came anyway. Repent to the Lord, and He will forgive and cleanse you. Let your heart turn from the sin and to God's truth and freedom. Humble yourself before God.
- Next, you need to flee or resist the enemy. The scripture tells us to flee sexual immorality/lust and to flee sin at first sight. That is what Joseph did with Potiphar's wife and what David should have done with Bathsheba and Uriah, her husband. The Bible tells us to resist the enemy, to stand firm on God's Word and truth, and to be immovable on the things of God. Do not entertain that thought or sin for a second. Run! Take that thought captive and cast it down (2 Corinthians 10:5). James 4:7–8 says to resist the enemy—after the first step of submitting to God—and he will flee.
- Then you need to draw near to God. When you have sought the Lord, repented, and resisted the enemy/temptation/sin, you can draw near to where God is showing the way out. Follow His lead; walk in the light of His truth. The Word says in Psalm 119, "Thy Word is a lamp unto my feet and a light unto my path." You need to let the Lord change and transform how you look at and how you normally respond to things/situations/circumstances/people. Your mind needs to be transformed and renewed to think like the Lord God Almighty. Set your mind on the things above in heaven. Do not focus on the situation but draw near to God. Instead of always looking for the bad, let God transform, teach, and show you how to grow through this trial. Let Him saturate your thoughts with His Word. His ways are higher, and His thoughts are higher than ours.
- Lastly, arm yourself:

  o Be filled with the Holy Spirit.
  o Walk in the Spirit.
  o Experience the baptism of the Holy Spirit.
  o Pray.

- Memorize the Word: Hide/engrave His Word on our hearts that we may not sin against Him.
- Put on the whole armor of God.
- Worship and get in His presence daily.
- Study the Word of God diligently to show thyself approved.

Sin no longer has dominion over me or you. Dominion means the power or right of governing and controlling; sovereign authority; rule; control; domination; a territory, usually of considerable size, in which a single rulership holds sway (www.dictionary.com). So through Jesus Christ, sin no longer has dominion or power over you and me. We have been given victory through His blood, death, resurrection, and through His Word and promises. He has made our way of escape! He is our way of escape!

Also, God is faithful. He has given us the resurrection power of the Holy Spirit to dwell within us, who is greater than those in the world or of the world. He is greater than Satan, who is trying to tempt us and cause us to fall (1 John 4:4). God, in His faithfulness, has given us victory over everything the enemy tries to throw at us. Take the way out that God is giving you. Do not fall into the trap of the enemy. Run, flee temptation, run to Jesus. Surrender every desire to Him and get victory over it!

> Little children (believers, dear ones), you are of God and you belong to Him and have [already] overcome them [the agents of the antichrist]; because He who is in you is greater than he (Satan) who is in the world [of sinful mankind]. (1 John 4:4 AMP)

REFRESHING IN THE WATERFALL

*N*ow even though this was something the Lord showed me in 2015, it can apply at all times as we walk into the new things God has for us.

As my husband and I were praying this particular morning, the Lord showed me a picture and spoke to me. I saw a waterfall flowing freely from above with no beginning. On one side of the waterfall was 2014, the old thing; on the other side was 2015, the new thing God has for us. As we walked through the waterfall, we were refreshed, renewed, and free from all the bondage, baggage, whatever from 2014. We were washed anew, a fresh beginning this year, washed through the blood of Jesus. It was so refreshing. As I chose to walk through the waterfall, I felt things fall off me, and they did not follow me through the waterfall of Jesus flowing over me. It was a beautiful experience.

So full of hope and the promise of the Lord Jesus Christ, God Almighty, we walked in a new freedom this year from everything that tried to hang on to us last year. When we wash, we rid ourselves of all the dirt and grime of the day and particles of the atmosphere we worked in. We feel clean. In the same way, when Jesus washes us daily with His blood, He removes the sins, dirt, heaviness, oppression, tiredness, and frustration of the times we are going through. Refresh means to give new strength or energy to reinvigorate, stimulate, or jog someone's memory by checking or going over previous information. Similarly, when the wind of the Holy Spirit refreshes us, He gives us new strength and energy to reinvigorate us to walk into the new things of God.

To refresh is also the Holy Spirit reminding us of the promises and faithfulness of God and His truth as He stimulates our memories of the words God has spoken over us. Renew means to resume an activity after an interruption, to reestablish, give fresh life, or strengthen something that is broken or worn-out to extend its validity. It's the same with the Holy Spirit of God. He reestablishes us to help us resume our walk with the Lord after an enemy attack might have tried to interrupt us. He gives us fresh life and strength and revives us and replaces/repairs those things that may have been broken in us from the issues of life or that tried to wear us out.

Do you find yourself being weighed down by too many burdens, unable to move because of guilt and shame?

Do you find you need to be refreshed and renewed by the power of the Holy Spirit reminding you who you are and whose you are?

Are you holding on to unforgiveness with someone because they hurt you deeply? Or you messed up royally and need to seek someone else's forgiveness?

What baggage is keeping you from the new things God has ready for you to walk into?

Give it to Jesus.

Lay it at His feet.

Let go of the past, and

Walk into the refreshing waterfall of the Holy Spirit to strengthen you to move forward into all the new freedom and blessings of the Lord Jesus Christ.

Following are some scriptures to uplift and renew your strength and faith for the new that God has for you, for us all.

> And may the Lord make you increase and abound in love to one another and to all, just as we do to you, so that He May establishes your hearts blameless in holiness before our God and Father at the coming of our Lord Jesus Christ with all His saints. (1 Thessalonians 3:12–13 NKJV)

> Now may the God of peace Himself sanctify you completely; and may your whole spirit, soul, and body be preserved blameless at the coming of our Lord Jesus Christ. He who calls you is faithful, who also will do it. (1 Thessalonians 5:23–24 NKJV)

> For the love of Christ compels us, because we judge thus: that if One died for all, then all died; and He died for all, that those who live should live no longer for themselves, but for Him who died for them and rose again. (2 Corinthians 5:14–15 NKJV)

Beloved, I pray that you may prosper in all things and be in health, just as your soul prospers. (3 John 1:2 NKJV)

Cast all your burden upon the Lord and He will sustain you; He will never allow the righteous to be shaken. (Psalm 55:22 NASB)

Now may the God of hope fill you with all joy and peace in believing, that you may abound in hope by the power of the Holy Spirit. (Romans 15:13 NKJV)

Rejoicing in hope, patient in tribulation, continuing steadfastly in prayer. (Romans 12:12 NKJV)

God is our refuge and strength, a very present help in trouble. Therefore we will not fear, even though the earth be removed, and though the mountains be carried into the midst of the sea; though its waters roar and be troubled, though the mountains shake with its swelling ... Be still and know that I am God; I will be exalted among the nations, I will be exalted in the earth! (Psalm 46:1–3, 10 NKJV)

Afflicted city, storm-battered, unpitied: I'm about to rebuild you with stones of turquoise, lay your foundations with sapphires, construct your towers with rubies, your gates with jewels, and all your walls with precious stones. All your children will have God for their teacher—what a mentor for your children! You'll be built solid, grounded in righteousness, far from any trouble—nothing to fear! Far from terror—it won't even come close! If anyone attacks you, don't for a moment suppose that I sent them, and if any should attack, nothing will come of it. I create the blacksmith who fires up his forge and makes a weapon designed to kill. I also create the destroyer—but no weapon that can hurt you has ever been forged. Any accuser who takes you to court will be dismissed as a liar. This is what God's servants can expect. I'll see to it that everything works out for the best. God's decree. (Isaiah 54:11–17 MSG)

For your Maker is your husband, the Lord of hosts is His name; and your Redeemer is the Holy One of Israel; He is called the God of the whole earth ... In righteousness you shall be established; you shall be far from oppression, for you shall not fear; and from terror, for it shall not come near you. Indeed they shall surely assemble, but not because of Me. Whoever assembles against you shall fall for your sake. (Isaiah 54:5, 14–15 NJKV)

God rescued us from dead-end alleys and dark dungeons. He's set us up in the kingdom of the Son He loves so much, the Son who got us out of the pit we were in, got rid of the sins we were doomed to keep repeating. (Colossians 1:13–14 MSG)

You are of God, little children, and have overcome them, because He who is in you is greater than he who is in the world. (1 John 4:4 NKJV)

The Lord is my Rock and my Fortress and my Deliverer; my God, my strength, in whom I will trust; my shield and the horn of my salvation, my stronghold. I will call upon the Lord, who is worthy to be praised; so shall I be saved from my enemies ... In my distress I called upon the Lord, and cried out to my God; He heard my voice from His temple, and my cry came before Him even to His ears ... For You will light my lamp; the Lord my God will enlighten my darkness. For by You I can run against a troop, by my God I can leap over a wall. As for God, His way is perfect; the word of the Lord is proven; He is a shield to all who trust in Him. For who is God, except the Lord? And who is a rock, except our God? It is God who arms me with strength, and makes my way perfect. He makes my feet like the feet of deer, and sets me on my high places. He teaches my hands to make war, so that my arms can bend a bow of bronze. You have also given me the shield of Your salvation; Your right hand has held me up, Your gentleness has made me great. You enlarged my path under me, so my feet did not slip. I have pursued by enemies and overtaken them; neither did I turn back again till they were destroyed. I have wounded them, so that they could not rise; they have fallen under my

DONNA MCMILLIN

feet. For You have armed me with strength for the battle; You have subdued under me those who rose up against me. (Psalm 18:2–3, 6, 28–39 NKJV)

Blessed be the God and Father of our Lord Jesus Christ, who has blessed us with every spiritual blessing in the heavenly places in Christ. (Ephesians 1:3 NKJV)

(Definitions from www.dictionary.com.)

RESUSCITATE ME

*W*hen someone's heart stops, they stop breathing. We do CPR on them to try to resuscitate them and get their heart going and their lungs breathing again. Compression paddles are made to put enough shock on the heart to get it beating again. And as the heart starts to pump again, breath will come back to the person, and blood will once again flow through their body.

An illness, accident, or injury can cause a heart to stop. How much damage is done to the heart depends on the time frame between when the heart has stopped beating and it starts beating again. This can also determine the condition in which the person may live the rest of their life. Once the person's heart has started beating again and they are breathing, surgery might be necessary.

Spiritually, we can begin to experience a heart that does not beat or desire as much of God as it used to. We can become dull in our walk with the Lord if we tend to neglect our time with Jesus or our time in the Word. Or we can become weary because of what we have experienced in day-to-day life. Whatever it may be that causes our spiritual hearts to stop beating for the One who loves us, who created us, it is time for the Holy Spirit to resuscitate us, to do spiritual CPR on our hearts, minds, souls, and spirits. If not, we will begin to experience spiritual death, and our living breath from God will begin to seep out of us. We need Him to get our hearts beating for God again and His life-giving Word and Spirit to restore us to the place His life flows out of us, and we hunger for the Lord more than anything else. Let the Holy Spirit do spiritual CPR on our hearts and resuscitate us once again with His life-giving power and breath!

What areas of your walk with the Lord need a Holy Spirit shock to restore life?

Do you need to be resuscitated to experience deeper desires for God's presence and power in your life or marriage?

Does your prayer life need new life?

Resuscitate me, Holy Spirit of God.

Let Your rivers of living water flow deep from within my belly and out to bring life into others.

Resuscitate me, Holy Spirit of God, as Your vessel to bring life—Your life—wherever I go.

Breathe Your breath of life into me.

GOD'S TEMPLE

When I was in the US Marine Corps and stationed in Hawaii, I went to the beach when I first got there and got badly sunburned. My master sergeant pulled me into his office and told me that he could write me up because of damage to government property. You see, when you are in the marines (and I guess any branch of service), you are the property of the US government, and your body is not your own. He wanted to make sure I got this principle in my head so I would not do anything damaging to my body again. He wrote me up temporarily and said if I straightened up and did right, he would take it out after a while. He did remove it because I learned that lesson.

This reminded me that as a daughter of the King, as a Christian, a follower of Jesus Christ, I am no longer my own. I was bought with a price, a high price—the blood of Jesus. I am no longer a slave to sin, but I am not my own. I am God's. This body of mine (and yours as a child of God) is the temple of the Holy Spirit. He dwells in this body, and whatever I subject myself to, I am also subjecting the Holy Spirit of God to. I need to respect this body and use it to glorify God in everything that I do. I gladly lay my life down since Jesus paid such a high price for me, the ultimate price of laying down His life for me. Take care of your body and spirit. Whatever you allow in through the mouth or through the eyes or heart or ears for that matter, let it all be glorifying to God.

Do you see yourself as the temple of the Holy Spirit of God? Look at the scripture below. What does it say about your body? What does it mean when it says your body is the temple of the Holy Spirit?

What was the price Jesus paid for you?

Are the shows you watch on television or music you listen to glorify God or do they build up the flesh? Do they encourage you to walk closer with the Lord or encourage you in the things of the world?

Or do you not know that your body is the temple of the Holy Spirit who is in you, whom you have from God, and you are not your own? For you were bought at a price; therefore glorify God in your body and in your spirit, which are God's. (1 Corinthians 6:19–20 NKJV)

BUILDING THE TEMPLE OF GOD

As I was praying at church today, Saturday, January 16, 2016, the Holy Spirit began to give me some insight regarding building a place that is inviting to the presence of God and our body, the temple of the Holy Spirit of God Almighty.

When Solomon built the temple, he used the finest gold, silver, and so on, the finest materials to build the temple where the Spirit of the living God would dwell. He was building a temple worthy of housing the presence of God, the holiest of holies, where nothing undefiled could come in. Thinking about our temple—our bodies—where the Spirit of the living God lives, we need to build it with an awe and a holiness so it will be a place where the Holy Spirit would want to dwell, where He would not be offended but would be welcomed. Where He would not be repulsed but where He would be pleased to enter.

When our bodies or houses are filled with offense, bitterness, jealousy, anger, and so on to the point where we can no longer see clearly, we have not truly prepared a place for the Holy Spirit. We cannot allow anything defiled to enter this temple of our bodies. We should be more aware of what we allow in and look at our bodies and ask, "Am I building this temple so the presence of God and His holiness can or would want to dwell here, where He is welcomed?" Are we giving Him our best? Is this place of our temple, our body, inviting to the Lord, or does its contents repel Him? I want to build my body to make room for the Spirit of God, welcoming Him in to have His way in my life to bring glory to the Father in all I do and say.

Yes, I know we are not perfect, but He commands us to be holy for He is holy. And if God gives us the command, then He has also given us the power and strength through the Holy Spirit living in us to be able to be holy as He is holy. This holy does not mean perfect; it means sacred, pure, blameless, separated, godlikeness, God's innermost nature, set apart for and reserved for God and His service. We have been made blameless through the blood of Jesus that washes us white as snow. And God sent His Holy Spirit to live within us. The same power of the Holy Spirit who raised Jesus from the dead lives in us to give us the power to live holy lives.

The fruit of the Holy Spirit is love, joy, peace, long-suffering, kindness, goodness, faithfulness, gentleness, and self-control. Galatians 5:16–17 tells us to walk in the Spirit of God, and we will not fulfill the lust of the flesh; we will not walk in fleshly lust or desires. It also states our fleshly desires are always at war, battling the Spirit of God living within us. So we are constantly in a tug-of-war with our flesh and the Spirit of God. If we submit to and walk in the things and ways of God, the Spirit of God will win the battle inside us and cause us to reproduce the fruit of the Spirit in our lives. We cannot push the fruit of the Holy Spirit out. It automatically flows out of us when the Holy Spirit is in control of our entire being, thoughts, minds, hearts, actions, words, desires, wills, and so on.

So how do we build the temple of God in us instead of allowing our flesh to be in control? First, we must submit all our ways, thoughts, and desires to God. We must acknowledge that His ways and thoughts are a lot better and higher than our ways and thoughts. We need to give the Holy Spirit full control, and let God have it all. We need to read God's Word to know His truth sets us free. God's Word will reveal to us the way to live a life pleasing to the Lord. Then, His Word gets into our spirits and minds, renewing our minds and the way we think. We need to seek God in prayer and dwell in His presence daily, seeking His guidance and His power to live in obedience to His Word of truth. Release control. Let it go. God is better at life than we are, so let Him begin to build His temple in you.

What fruit of the Spirit is lacking in your life? Do you lack joy in your life? Do you love others like Jesus loves? Do you have peace deep down in your heart and mind? Do you offer kindness and gentleness to those you think are undeserving or who treat you badly? Do you allow self-control to rule or your desires of the flesh to take over?

What do you need to surrender to give the Holy Spirit full control of areas in your life that you have tried to control?

Pray and ask the Holy Spirit to show you the areas in your life and heart you need to surrender for Him to build His temple in you.

I say then: walk in the Spirit, and you shall not fulfill the lust of the flesh. For the flesh lusts against the Spirit, and the Spirit against the flesh: and these are contrary to one another, so that you do not do the things that you wish. (Galatians 5:16–17 NKJV)

But the fruit of the Spirit is love, joy, peace, long suffering, kindness, goodness, faithfulness, gentleness, self-control. Against such there is no law. And those who are Christ's have crucified the flesh with its passions and desires. (Galatians 5:22–24 NKJV)

Or do you not know that your body is the temple of the Holy Spirit who is in you, whom you have from God, and you are not your own? For you were bought at a price; therefore glorify God in your body and in your spirit, which are God's. (1 Corinthians 6:19–20 NKJV)

You are of God, little children, and have overcome them, because He who is in you is greater than he who is in the world. (1 John 4:4 NKJV)

Therefore submit to God. Resist the devil and he will flee from you. Draw near to God and He will draw near to you. Cleanse your hands, you sinners; and purify your hearts, you double-minded. (James 4:7–8 NKJV)

THE GOD WHO SEES

Then she called the name of the Lord who spoke to her, You-Are-the-God-Who-Sees; for she said, "Have I also here seen Him who sees me?" (Genesis 16:13 NKJV)

*J*ust a little background on this verse. Hagar was Sarah's maid, a bond servant given to her by her parents when she married Abraham. God had told Abraham that He would give him a child through Sarah, and his descendants would be great. During the time of waiting, Sarah had not conceived, so in trying to do things her way, she gave Hagar to Abraham to go and have a child. Hagar conceived and began to look down on her mistress, Sarah, because she conceived when Sarah could not. Sarah got angry and was probably even jealous, confused, and hurt. She demanded Abraham send Hagar away. Abraham told Sarah to do as she saw fit, so Sarah dealt harshly with Hagar. Hagar decided to run away because of the harshness of her mistress. The verse above is from the time of Hagar running away.

When Hagar ran from Sarah, I imagine that as she was out in the desert, she felt all alone with no one to help her or stand up for her. She had no close relatives nearby to go to, and I imagine she began to feel helpless. Then, the angel of the Lord appeared to Hagar and asked her where she had come from and where she was going. Hagar knew where she came from but did not know where she would go. God knew the answer to both questions. Hagar stopped to rest, and that is when she heard the voice of God. He told Hagar to return to her mistress and submit to her. But that was not all. God told her He would multiply her descendants too. She realized God is the God who sees us no matter what place we are in, no matter where we try to run, and no matter where we hide. God sees us and cares for us. God gave her instructions to guide her back to where she needed to be. God does the same for us. But it was in a place of rest that Hagar was able to see and hear God speaking to her.

Do you find yourself in that place of feeling like you are alone? Are you running away from something? Are you hiding from things in life? Do you find yourself in the wilderness? Have you made choices that go against God's Word and are now walking in those consequences? If so, know our God and Savior, Jesus Christ, is the God who sees you! He sees your heart, your hurts, your needs, your desires, and your brokenness. And He cares! Sometimes, in our darkest hours, we cannot see straight. We need to quiet ourselves to hear His voice. The Lord will appear to us and ask us questions to bring us back to where we can hear and see Him.

You are not alone. Your heavenly Father sees you and is with you. You have not messed up so badly that you cannot repent and turn back to Him. He will receive you again. No matter where we go, the Bible says that we cannot get out of His presence or sight. In Romans 8, Paul tells us nothing can separate us from His love. God is reaching out to you to guide you back to where you need to be. He is letting you know when you follow Him and His guidance, He will provide for you. He will take care of you. He will protect you. He will comfort you. He will give you His peace, and He will bless and multiply you!

Jesus is calling out to you right now. Lift up your head and hear Him calling your name. Follow His voice for He sees you wherever you are, and He loves you. Stop running! Quiet yourself to listen for His voice, and be obedient to Him.

See Genesis 16; Psalm 139; Romans 8.

DONNA MCMILLIN

CLEANSE OUR HEARTS

*I*n Ezekiel chapters 8 and 10, God lifts Ezekiel up in the Spirit and takes him to Jerusalem to the gates of the inner court. God tells Ezekiel to look inside a hole/door in the inner court—where they brought their sacrifices to the Lord—and allows Ezekiel to see what is happening in the inner courts. Ezekiel sees all kinds of sins and the worship of all kinds of idols in the inner court.

As I read this, I could feel the disgust of what Ezekiel saw and how it must hurt the heart of God to see His people worshipping other idols in His temple. Then I thought of how God looks on the inside of us, inside every room of our hearts, and wondered, *What does He see or find there?* Does He see any idols we have put before Him, or does He see our hearts clean and totally devoted to Him? Daily, we must let the Lord search our hearts and see if there is anything we have allowed to enter that needs to be cleansed with the blood of Jesus.

Jeremiah 17:9 says, "The heart is deceitful above all things, and desperately wicked; who can know it."

Proverbs 4:23 says, "Keep your heart with all diligence, for out of it springs the issues of life."

Psalm 139:23–24 says, "Search me, O God, and know my heart; try me and know my anxieties and see if there is any wicked way in me, and lead me in the way everlasting."

God wants our hearts totally devoted, surrendered, and committed to Him. We cannot trust our own hearts at times because they are deceitful and can lead us away from the Lord. So, we need to do as David did in Psalm 51:7 and 10. David had sinned, committing adultery and murder, and was confronted with his sins. David did not try to hide them or his heart before God because he understood God knows our hearts and all that is within them. David asked God in verse 7 to "Purge me with hyssop, and I shall be clean; wash me, and I shall be whiter than snow." Back then, hyssop was part of Israelites bringing their sacrifices to God to be cleansed of their sins. David knew if God purged and washed him, then he would be totally clean and whiter than snow.

David did not stop there. In verse 10, David asks God to "Create in me a clean heart, O God, and renew a steadfast spirit within me." In Matthew Henry's commentary says David asked God to create in him a clean heart because God is the One who creates, and only God can permanently create a clean heart in us through the blood of Jesus. Also Matthew Henry's commentary defines renew as God repairing the decay of spiritual strength that this sin has caused and setting it to right again.

It makes me understand and see how 2 Corinthians 5:17 applies so graciously to us as we ask God to create in us a clean heart and renew a steadfast spirit within us. It can only be done through faith in Jesus Christ and His blood. Second Corinthians 5:17 states, "Therefore if anyone is in Christ, he is a new creation; old things have passed away; behold, all things have become new." When we approach God as David did, trusting Jesus as Savior and Lord of our lives and believing His blood was shed for our sins and cleanses us once and for all, then God the Creator makes all things become new in us, new ways of thinking, being, doing, and living.

Proverbs 4:23 says, "to keep our hearts with all diligence." We do this by seeking God diligently with our hearts, souls, minds, and spirits, and by loving Him with all our hearts, souls, minds, and strengths, leaving space for nothing but Jesus. We must seek Jesus first, above all, desiring His will be done and not our own, dying to our flesh, and pursuing His ways and His truths. Let God search our hearts continually (Psalm 139:23–24), get out anything that is not of Him, and lead us in His everlasting way: "Purge me and I shall be clean, wash me and I shall be whiter than snow!" Praise You, Jesus!

We can invite God to examine our hearts with us. We can trust Jesus to see our hearts truly, and we include Him because sometimes, when we investigate on our own, we may see things—good and bad—that are not truly there. Jesus knows our hearts better than we do. So let us invite Him in to search our hearts with us truthfully and clearly.

And remember, in Christ Jesus, we are a new creation. Old things have passed away. Behold, all things become new. Especially remember that when the enemy tries to remind you of your past, those old things are permanently gone. You are a new creation in Christ Jesus, so stand. Let us

DONNA MCMILLIN

abide in Jesus, letting Him abide in us continually. There we find cleansing and wholeness, newness of life, hope and joy, and peace everlasting. You will find your heart, soul, and mind refreshed.

For further discussion, see Ezekiel chapters 8–10; Jeremiah 17:9; 23:13; Deuteronomy 4:29; 6:5; 10:12; 30:6; Joel 2:12; Joshua 22:5; Psalms 16:11; 51:7, 10; 139:23–24; Proverbs 4:23; Matthew 22:37; Luke 10:27; Mark 12:30; John 15:4–5, 7, 10; Acts 3:19; 2 Corinthians 5:17. See also *Matthew Henry Commentary* on Ezekiel, chapters 8–10.

DYING TO SELF

Most assuredly, I say to you, unless a grain of wheat falls into the ground and dies, it remains alone; but if it dies, it produces much grain. He who loves his life will lose it, and he who hates his life in this world will keep it for eternal life. (John 12:24–25 NKJV)

A farmer knows when he plants a little seed of wheat, it is just one little seed in the ground, but it can grow and transform into an abundant crop to feed hundreds and thousands of people. Once planted, the seed begins to die. Then as it is watered and fed, it grows up out of the ground and does not even look like the seed that was planted. This is the same way with us. The seed of truth in Jesus Christ, the Son of God as our Savior and Lord, is planted in our hearts the minute we believe in Him. Then, as we begin to seek the Lord, spend time in prayer and in His presence, and let His word of truth transform us and renew our minds to think like Him, we begin to grow more into His image. But our images must die to do this. When we are transformed, we begin to look more like God every day. It is a lifetime process.

John the Baptist said, "He must increase, I must decrease," talking about Jesus. Jesus says repeatedly in scripture that we must deny ourselves and pick up our cross to follow Him. In Matthew 10:28, Jesus even says if we do not take up our cross and follow Him, we are not worthy of Him. The cross is a symbol of death. So Jesus is telling us to pick up our cross, our cross of dying to self and living for Him. Our cross of dying to our desires and letting His desires fill us. That is not easy. Not at all. Because Jesus has given us the Holy Spirit, His resurrection power living within us, it is attainable but only through Him. It is a daily process because our flesh wants to do what it wants to do.

Galatians 5:16–17 says, "Walk in the Spirit, and you shall not fulfill the lust of the flesh. For the flesh lusts against the Spirit, and the Spirit against the flesh; and these are contrary to one another, so that you do not do the things that you wish." There is always going to be a battle going on, but God has given us, through His divine power and Holy Spirit within us, all things that pertain to life and godliness through the knowledge of Jesus. We have everything we need in Jesus to live a life of godliness (2 Peter 1:3).

We are to put off the old man of sin and corruption and put on the new man in Christ Jesus for a new life. Those who are in Christ Jesus are new creations; the old things have passed away. Behold all things have become new (2 Corinthians 5:17). We must break agreement with lust, greed, power, envy, jealousy, lying, hatred, sexual impurity of any kind, gossip, and racism—the old man before Christ. Transformation comes as we die to self and allow the Holy Spirit to have control. We then open the door for the fruit of the Spirit—love, joy, peace, long-suffering, kindness, goodness, faithfulness, gentleness, and self-control—to flow out of us (Galatians 5:22–23). And Galatians 5:24 says, "And those who are Christ's have crucified the flesh with its passions and desires." We walk by the Spirit of God as new creations in Christ Jesus, dying to ourselves, the old man, and living as the new man in Christ Jesus by His power in us. If this were not possible, Jesus would not have told us this. But we can do all things through Christ who strengthens us (Philippians 4:13). Also, His grace is sufficient for us for His strength is made perfect in our weakness (2 Corinthians 12:9).

Ask the Lord what things you still need to die to. Then pray and ask Him to give you the strength to put off the old man and let the new man in Him become your life.

It is not easy, but the eternal rewards are better than anything our flesh or this world has to offer.

FRAGRANCE OF JESUS CHRIST

$\mathcal{W}$hen He sacrificed Himself on the cross, Christ Jesus was a sweet-smelling aroma to God. When Christ died, the aroma of His sacrifice reached the nostrils of God in heaven, and God was pleased with Him. God then applied His blood sacrifice toward us for the ultimate sacrifice for sin and death once and for all.

Ephesians 5:1–2 tells us, "be imitators of God … walk[ing] in love as Christ has loved us and gave Himself for us, an offering and a sacrifice to God for a sweet-smelling aroma." So, as we imitate Jesus walking in love toward others, we too become a sweet-smelling aroma to those around us and to God. We emit the fragrance of Christ when we imitate the love He demonstrated when He gave Himself up for us.

Second Corinthians 2:14–16 says that through us God diffuses the fragrance of His knowledge in every place we go. To Him, we are the fragrance of Christ to the saved and the lost who are perishing. To the saved, it is a fragrance of life leading to life. But to the lost who are perishing, it is a fragrance of death leading to death. That means some will receive and cherish His fragrance and knowledge we leave with them. Some will not and possibly come against us or attack us verbally or physically.

A fragrance has a pleasant smell. I think about perfumes, cologne, flowers, baking sweets, or cooking smells. These can emit wonderful and delicious fragrances as we breathe them in. But there are also smells that do not smell so sweet, like spoiled food, body odor after a hard workout, bathrooms that have not been cleaned in a while, and the sweaty smelly odors of onions, fire, dead animals, and animal or human waste. These are offensive to our nostrils when we breathe them in.

I think about my friend and pastor's wife, Cathy, who wears perfume. She always leaves her fragrance wherever she has walked, and it smells great. I don't mind that smell. But then, I think about our church when we used to begin preparations for our Fall Festival. We had a day of cutting up two thousand pounds of onion rings. At the beginning, we would leave the onions in our church kitchen or cut them up in the church kitchen. And wow, when we came to church the next day, the whole church smelled of sweaty smelly onions. This was not a great smell, and it lingered for quite some time. In either of those examples, if we spend any amount of time around those smells, the fragrance can begin to come on and out of us.

As we spend time with Jesus and the fellowship of Holy Spirit, His fragrance pours out on us. The more time we spend with Him in His presence, the stronger His sweet-smelling aroma gets on us and flows from us wherever we go. When we leave the presence of God to go about our day, we have the ability to leave the fragrance of Christ everywhere we walk, to settle there in the place and in people's hearts.

I think about Peter and Paul, how even their shadows or handkerchiefs carried the fragrance of Christ, and thus, carried the healing power of Christ. I think about Stephen who did great signs, miracles, and wonders. As Stephen was declaring the knowledge of Jesus to the Jews at the council, it was said his face shown as the face of an angel. But as Stephen began to talk more, scripture says the Jews were cut to the heart and began gnashing at and stoning him. Stephen was still being the aroma of Jesus as he spoke, but this was the crowd of the perishing, and it was to them the aroma of death. Instead of receiving it, they rejected it and killed Stephen.

But standing at the place was Saul, who would later be converted to Paul by the revelation of Jesus on the road to Damascus. Maybe to Saul, the fragrance of Christ coming from Stephen was not good at first. But because of the witness of Stephen, I believe the fragrance of Christ in Stephen became the aroma of life leading to life in Paul.

We are to live like the church in the book of Acts. Spending time in prayer with the Lord and in His presence causes where we are to shake. As we go out into our jobs, our homes, stores, our lives, our families, we carry the fragrance of Jesus Christ—His love, His laying down His life for us—as we sacrifice time in our lives for others, as we touch those who are hurting, as we comfort those who are broken or lost loved ones, and as we share the knowledge of God our Savior, Jesus Christ, to a hurting world. Remember, to the saved, it is an aroma leading to life. But to the lost and perishing, it is an aroma of death leading to death. So some will receive, and some will reject. But no matter what, we carry the fragrance of the sweet-smelling aroma of Christ to others. Then rivers of living water will flow out of us, touching lives, turning the world upside down, and building the kingdom of God here on earth as it is in heaven.

I see it happening in my church. People are on fire, speaking the knowledge of God, flowing in His power and by His Spirit, and speaking truth and love to coworkers. They come to church filled with His fragrance and emit His aroma in our services. I am excited because I believe each new year we will begin to see and smell more of the sweet-smelling aroma and fragrance of Christ Jesus flowing out of His people into this earth and our families, neighborhoods, cities, and nations.

What fragrance do you carry into situations, your job, or home? Is it a sweet-smelling aroma of Jesus's love and forgiveness, or is it the stench of bitterness, hatred, or unforgiveness?

What areas of your daily life need the refreshing, sweet-smelling aroma of Jesus to bring healing and wholeness?

Pray and ask the Lord to help you to carry His fragrance into situations and into the lives of others so they can see Jesus's love through you.

See 2 Corinthians 2:14–16; Ephesians 5:1–2; John 7:36.

LOOK BEYOND THE SURFACE

I heard the Lord say to me at the beginning of the year 2020, "Do not determine this year by the things we see; do not judge this year by what is happening." We can apply this to every year we walk into and in everything going on in this world today.

So, with that, I saw a picture on Facebook where it expressed 2020 as a beehive piñata, meaning when hit, it would let loose a hive of attacking bees. Then I saw the next post from a Christian organization that said, "Be watchful, be on the alert," and something about prayer.

As soon as I saw that, my spirit agreed. Yes, this year, 2020, has been one thing after another, just like a bombardment against us. Amid this, I felt the Holy Spirit telling me, "Look beyond what you see; be watchful. Look beyond what you see to see and hear what God is doing in the midst of it all, what God is wanting to do in us." It was almost like what has been happening on this earth was like a curtain, but God wanted us to be faithful, curious even, and have the wisdom to look beyond the curtain to see what is really going on in the spiritual realm and what He really wants to do through us and through it all.

You know, when there is a play on a stage, there is a curtain behind the actors hiding all kinds of activities being done to prepare for the next scene or to help the actors through a scene. Likewise, there are things behind the scenes of this spiritual curtain (COVID-19, racial issues, the economy, and so on) trying to push against truth and righteousness. But also behind the scenes are those who are trying to establish God's truth and righteousness through it all. So we have to push past this curtain to see what is really going on and then get the right perspective on how to fight and how to pray.

Two types of curtains exist: the one that closes after a scene as the actors scatter around to get to their next places/scenes/costumes, and the curtain that closes when the play is finished. With the first curtain, our job as the church is to stop the scattering actors through prayer, replacing them with a host of heaven's army, the actors of God's truth and righteousness. We must change what is going on behind the curtain so that when the final curtain is closed, God will reign victorious in this nation.

Christians must diligently look beyond what is going on to see the hand of God moving in and through this. We must purposefully seek what God wants of the church. In transforming the church, we can turn the world upside down with the faith of His power moving even amid all this chaos. Above all, we must be more prayerful to see God's wisdom and understanding of the times and to know what to do in these times. We must be determined, no matter what, to push past the curtain of what is happening in the natural to see what God is doing spiritually. And we must stand, having done all to stand, in God's truth, righteousness, and faithfulness, believing He will not just get us through this but wants to do a great move in and through us. Put on the full armor of God and let us go to fight this battle with Him leading and being our rear guard. He is the Lord God, the Host of heaven's army.

Are you seeing only what is happening in the natural world today? Or can you see beyond the natural to see what God is doing or wants to do in these times?

Ask the Lord to remove any scales or veils over your eyes and off your ears to see Him and hear His voice more clearly.

Pray for the anointing of the sons of Issachar, the anointing to understand the times and know what to do in them. Ask the Lord what you need to be doing in these times.

> Therefore he sent horses and chariots and a great army there, and they came by night and surrounded the city. And when the servant of the man of God arose early and went out, there was an army, surrounding the city with horses and chariots. And his servant said to him, "alas, my master! What shall we do?" So he answered, "do not fear, for those who are with us are more than those who are with them." And Elisha prayed, and said, "Lord, I pray, open his eyes that he may see." Then the Lord opened the eyes of the young man, and he saw. And behold, the mountain was full of horses and chariots of fire all around Elisha. (2 Kings 6:14–17 NKJV)

If you read the rest of this story, you will see God blinded the enemy's army and led them into the town to be captured.

> For thus says the Lord of hosts, the God of Israel: "houses and field and vineyards shall be possessed again in this land." (Jeremiah 32:15 NKJV)

> By faith Noah, being warned by God about things not yet see, in reverence prepared an ark for the salvation of his household, by which he condemned the world, and became an heir of the righteousness which is according to faith. (Hebrews 11:7 NASB)

> But you be watchful in all things, endure afflictions, do the work of an evangelist, fulfill your ministry. (2 Timothy 4:5 NKJV)

> But the end of all things is at hand; therefore be serious and watchful in your prayers. (1 Peter 4:7 NKJV)

> Be sober, be vigilant; because your adversary the devil walks about like a roaring lion, seeking who he may devour. (1 Peter 5:8 NKJV)

> Devote yourselves to prayer, keeping alert in it with an attitude of thanksgiving; conduct yourselves with wisdom toward outsiders, making the most of the opportunity. Let your speech always be with grace, as though seasoned with salt, so that you will know how you should respond to each person. (Colossians 4:2 NASB)

DISCERNING SHADOWS

As I was out on my bike ride today, I suddenly saw the shadow of a flock of birds before I saw the actual birds. At first, I almost thought those birds were going to fly right into me. But then I thought, *Oh no, that is just their shadow.*

It reminded me of Psalms 23 and 91. And the Lord brought to mind a message my pastor preached a while back. I thought, *Now isn't that just like the devil to use a shadow of birds to bring fear up in me to swerve and possibly get hurt.* The enemy tries to use shadows of darkness, sicknesses, hurts, pains, sufferings, and other things coming against us to try to overshadow us and cause fear to rise. But the devil is a liar, as my friend Cathy says. Like Psalm 23 says, "shadow of death" is just a shadow, not the real thing.

Then I thought of another shadow, the shadow of God's great protection as we dwell in His secret place under His wings, our refuge and fortress (Psalm 91). In Him, we abide under His great shadow of refuge, healing, deliverance, protection, provision, hope, life, and peace. He covers us with His wings. His truth is our shield and buckler, reminding us it is just a mere shadow, and His truth sets us free so we can overcome.

Even when the enemy tries to bring his shadow over us, the Word of God says in Psalm 23, "You prepare a table before me in the presence of my enemies; You anoint my head with oil; my cup runs over. Surely goodness and mercy shall follow me all the days of my life; and I will dwell in the house of the Lord forever." In the Bible, oil usually represents the Holy Spirit. So just know, even in the presence of our enemies, God is anointing us with His oil, the oil of the Holy Spirit to overcome.

So, when the enemy comes with his shadow of darkness, we need not fear. Just remember the protection, power, and refuge under the shadow of our almighty God, and know that He has us! No fear. Even if we walk in the "shadow" of death, we will not fear because He is with us. In the presence of the enemy, He anoints our heads overflowing with His oil!

What shadows—fears, lies, hurts, pain—has the enemy tried to keep over you that you need to give to the Lord in order to be set free?

Are you allowing the enemy to overshadow the truth of God's Word in your life?

Are you trusting in the Lord for His shadow of protection or in your own power?

What promises of God can you speak and declare over your life to bring freedom from the lies of the enemy?

> Yea, though I walk through the valley of the shadow of death, I will fear no evil; for You are with me; Your rod and Your staff, they comfort me. You prepare a table before me in the presence of my enemies; You anoint my head with oil; My cup runs over. Surely goodness and mercy shall follow me all the days of my life; and I will dwell in the house of the Lord forever. (Psalm 23:4–6 NKJV)

> He who dwells in the secret place of the Most High shall abound under the shadow of the Almighty. I will say of the Lord, "He is my refuge and my fortress; my God, in Him I will trust." Surely He shall deliver you from the snare of the fowler and from the perilous pestilence. He shall cover you with His feathers, and under His wings you shall take refuge; His truth shall be your shield and buckler. You shall not be afraid of the terror by night, nor of the arrow that flies by day. (Psalm 91:1–5 NKJV)

JESUS, OUR HEALER

As He was approaching Jericho [on His way to Jerusalem], it happened that a blind man was sitting beside the road begging. Now when he heard a crowd going by, he began to ask what this was [about]. They told him, "Jesus of Nazareth is passing by." So, he shouted out, saying, "Jesus, Son of David (Messiah), have mercy on me!" Those who were leading the way were sternly telling him to keep quiet; but he screamed even more, "Son of David, have mercy on me!" Then Jesus stopped and ordered that the blind man be led to Him; and when he came near, Jesus asked him, "What do you want Me to do for you?" He said, "Lord, let me regain my sight!" Jesus said to him, "Regain your sight; your [personal trust and confident] faith [in Me] has made you well." Immediately he regained his sight and began following Jesus, glorifying and praising and honoring God. And all the people, when they saw it, praised God. (Luke 18:35-43 AMP)

And suddenly, a woman who had a flow of blood for twelve years came from behind and touched the hem of His garment. For she said to herself, "If only I may touch His garment, I shall be made well." But Jesus turned around, and when He saw her He said, "Be of good cheer, daughter; your faith has made you well." And the woman was made well from that hour. (Matthew 9:20–22 NKJV)

Jesus went to Capernaum to preach ... immediately many gathered together, so that there was no longer room to receive them, not even near the door. And He preached the word to them. Then they came to him bringing a paralytic who was carried by four men. And when they could not come near Him because of the crowd, they uncovered the roof where He was. So, when they had broken through, they let down the bed on which the paralytic was lying. When Jesus saw their faith, He said to the paralytic, "Son, your sins are forgiven you." (Mark 2:2–5)

DONNA MCMILLIN

Above, we have three healing encounters with Jesus. One who kept yelling, louder and louder, crying out to Jesus for healing even when the crowd told him to be quiet. The next told only herself what she was going to do as she came quietly behind Jesus to touch His garment to be healed. The third was a man unable to take himself to Jesus for healing but relied on four friends, who must have loved him greatly because of the lengths they were willing to go through for him. All received their healings. The first two had made up their minds they were going to seek Jesus and get their healings, while the third one had friends who were just as determined for him to receive his healing. All were determined to come before Him and not let anyone or anything stop them.

I always kind of chuckle when I read about the blind man. The people were telling him to be quiet, but he was like, "Hey, you don't know what it is to be blind. I'm going to cry out to Jesus even more so He can hear me above the crowd. You are not going to stop me from coming before Jesus and seeking my healing." He was very determined to stand before Jesus to get His attention, so he could ask for his healing. Jesus noticed him and called him to Him, asking the blind man what he wanted. The man told Jesus he wanted his eyesight back. Jesus told him, "Receive your sight; you are healed." In one of the Gospels, it says when Jesus called him, the blind man threw off the garment he was wrapped in. I think the garment represented all the years of being blind (the old man), and he was letting go of all the old and going to Jesus for his new life with sight.

I am somber when I read about the woman who suffered for twelve years with an issue of blood. She was tired. She had spent all her money on doctors, and after all the doctors' appointments, she was even worse off than at first. She was desperate and determined within herself she would receive her healing if she just touched the hem of Jesus's garment. So she set out to do just that. In a great crowd, she quietly approached Jesus from behind so as not to be noticed. She touched His garment and was immediately healed. Jesus turned, acknowledged this woman, and told her she was healed to confirm her healing even more. Maybe she wanted to come in under the radar and not be noticed because she dealt with shame from her illness. Having an issue of blood for twelve years was reason for her to have to call, "unclean" to all those she might have to encounter. The customs of the Jews would have put some shame on her. She just wanted to sneak in and get her healing without being recognized.

But I believe Jesus knew the shame she carried—because, come on, this is Jesus, and He knew who touched Him—and wanted to acknowledge her healing before all to break her shame and heal her physically, emotionally, and spiritually. She had to understand that when Jesus called her forward, there was compassion in His words, and He wanted her to be set free from all bondages.

Then, with joyful tears, I read about the paralytic who was unable to go to Jesus on his own for healing. But he had four friends who loved him enough to take him on his bed to see Jesus. They did not allow overcrowding to deter them from helping their friend receive his healing. They saw the roof and knew they could dig a hole through the roof and drop him down in front of Jesus, and Jesus would not be able to ignore their friend. Wow, to have friends like that who will go to whatever length they can to fight for your healing. Jesus saw the four friends' faith—not the faith of the paralytic man and because of their faith—He healed the paralytic and forgave him his sins.

These three unique ways of coming to Jesus show us that though we may be different and have different approaches and desperation to get to Jesus for our own healings, peace, comfort, wisdom, strength, guidance, He hears us all and responds with healing. Receive what you ask for in His name. The name above every name, Jesus. He hears and responds to our every cry, our every prayer, and our desperation as we call out to Him. Be encouraged. Don't give up. Don't be quiet. Don't back down. Keep asking, keep seeking, and keep knocking on the doors of heaven, and we will receive, we will find, and God will open doors to us that no man can shut! How desperate are you for your own healing and the healing of family members and loved ones? Enough to overshout the rising voices telling you that Jesus won't hear you or won't heal you? Enough to humble yourself and come to Him knowing He is your healer? Enough to trust friends to pray for you, bringing you before the throne room of heaven to seek your healing?

God is faithful!

Who forgives all your iniquities, and Who heals all your diseases. (Psalm 103:3 NKJV)

Who Himself bore our sins in His own body on the tree, that we, having died to sins, might live for righteousness—by whose stripes you were healed. (1 Peter 2:24 NKJV)

Is anyone among you sick? Let him call for the elders of the church, and let them pray over him, anointing him with oil in the name of the Lord. And the prayer of faith will save the sick, and the Lord will raise him up. And if he has committed sins, he will be forgiven. Confess your trespasses to one another, and pray for one another, that you may be healed. The effective, fervent prayer of a righteous man avails much. (James 5:14–16 NKJV)

That it might be fulfilled which was spoken by Isaiah the prophet, saying: "He Himself took our infirmities and bore our sicknesses." (Matthew 8:17 NKJV)

He sent His word and healed them, and delivered them from their destructions. (Psalm 107:20 NKJV)

THE ULTIMATE STANDARD
OF LIVING

What standard of living do we hold ourselves to? What standard of living do we hold our children, spouses, families, and nations to? As Christians, the only standard of living that we should hold ourselves to is God's standard of living.

When I talk about standard of living, I am talking about letting God's will be done spiritually, naturally, financially, and in every other area of our lives. God's standard of living is the highest, and it is achievable because He has given us His Holy Spirit—our Helper, teacher, counselor, steward, the Comforter, and so much more—to live inside us. I am certainly not referring to this world's standard of living. And if we are honest with ourselves, not our personal standard of living. I believe whatever standard of living we hold ourselves to, that is the standard of living we are going to get in our lives. If we hold ourselves to a lower standard of living, we will not expect much out of ourselves, our lives, or anyone else. But if we hold ourselves to a higher standard, God's standard of living, then we begin to thrive for a better way, a better life for ourselves and loved ones, and even a better country.

King David walked in integrity of heart and uprightness. God even called David a man after His own heart (1 Kings 9:4; 1 Samuel 13:14). Psalm 78:72 says David shepherded his people/nation according to the integrity of his heart and guided them by the skillfulness of his hands.

Joseph, when confronted with temptation of sexual impurity by Potiphar's wife throwing herself at him, chose God's standard of living and ran from the temptation (Genesis 39:7–12; 1 Corinthians 6:18). Phinehas stood for God's standard of living when he killed the Israelite man and his wife, a foreigner who worshipped idols and the gods of the land, because the man dare bring her to the door of the temple of the living Holy God (Numbers 25:1–13; Psalm 106:28–31).

Even Solomon built the temple according to God's standard and kept every item holy by using the best of the best. Job and Noah were also righteous men who lived by God's standard. And if you want to know more accounts and their rewards, all you need to do is read Hebrews 11, the faith chapter, and read about all the men and women who chose God's standard of living over the world's and their own standards of living.

Regarding our finances, I am not saying live above our means. But I am talking about a higher standard of giving, tithing, and of helping others and the church financially. God is clear; those who give sparingly receive sparingly, and those who give liberally receive liberally. Jim, my husband, and I are a living testimony to that truth of God's Word (2 Corinthians 9:6).

We must practice God's higher standard of living in our love, kindness, forgiveness, mercy, grace, goodness, long-suffering with others, and time spent with His people.

Jesus said many times, "you have heard it said, but I say," He was raising the standard for us in our walk with Him and in our witness of Him and His great goodness, love, forgiveness, mercy, grace, serving, sacrifice, comfort, purity, peace, strength, power, victory, and holiness on display for the world to see Jesus above all else in and through us.

So, let us begin to raise our standards to match God's standard of living. Then we can begin to experience the miracles, signs, and wonders Jesus says we will and can walk in with Him. And we can experience the breakthroughs He promises in our spiritual and natural lives, and even in our finances. Finally, we can see souls added to the Kingdom of God daily. Let's walk it out!

> You have heard that it was said to those of old, "you shall not commit adultery." But I say to you that whoever looks at a woman to lust for her has already committed adultery with her in his heart. (Matthew 5:27-28 NKJV)

> You have heard that it was said, "you shall love your neighbor and hate your enemy." But I say to you, love your enemies, bless those who curse you, do good to those who hate you, and pray for those who spitefully use you and persecute you, that you may be sons of your Father in heaven; for He makes His sun rise on the evil and on the good, and sends rain on the just and on the unjust. (Matthew 5:43–45 NKJV)

IDENTITY THEFT

One day last year, I heard the words "identity theft" as I was praying. I believe the Holy Spirit of God spoke those words.

Identity theft exists in the world, whether through the internet or other sources. But right now, in this world, there is another type of identity theft going on, and it is from the enemy of our souls. The enemy steals through identity and gender confusion, creating an all-out war on the hearts and souls of our children and young people, and probably even on older adults.

Our identity comes from who we are in Christ Jesus. He teaches us through His Word who we are and who He created us to be. His Word teaches that God made us male and female. His Word teaches males and females are to procreate and populate the earth. His Word teaches we are made in His image, in His likeness. His Word teaches we are victorious over the enemy of our souls, and we are more than conquerors in Him. His Word teaches we are blessed, we are made whole, we are light in the darkness, we are the salt of the earth, and we can boldly enter God's presence through the blood and righteousness of Jesus Christ. His Word teaches we are joint heirs with Christ Jesus, a holy people, a royal priesthood, a chosen generation, and God's special people to proclaim His praises. God's Word says He called us out of darkness into His glorious light. His Word teaches we are the head and not the tail, we are His church. His Word teaches He knew us before we were even formed in our mothers' wombs. He created us for a special purpose, and He wants to give us a future and a hope. His Word teaches we are blessed going out and coming in. His Word teaches us we have all the spiritual blessings in the heavens in Christ Jesus, and His divine power has given to us all things pertaining to life and godliness through the knowledge of Christ Jesus. His Word teaches us we can slay giants, tear down strongholds, run, jump over walls, overcome all the power of the enemy, and live a victorious life here on earth and eternal life through faith in Jesus Christ, our God and Savior. His Word teaches us He is the lifter of our heads, so we do not have to walk in shame anymore when we know Jesus as our Savior and Lord. His Word teaches us there is now no condemnation to those who are in Christ Jesus who do not walk according to the flesh but according to the Spirit of God. His Word teaches us if we confess our sins to Him, He is faithful and just to forgive us our sins and cleanse us from all unrighteousness. His Word teaches us that we are His workmanship, His creation created to glorify Him.

The enemy works through the world to bring confusion to people about who they are, wanting them to question their identities. The enemy wants them to question whether they are male or female or something else other than who God created them to be. The enemy wants to steal our identities, and we cannot let him. The world says you can be whoever you want to be. If you are created a female, the world says, "Oh no, you can be a male or vice versa." Or if you think you are an animal, the enemy is saying, "Sure, you can be an animal." The enemy wants us to be less than what God created us to be. The enemy, working through the world, wants us to doubt who and how God created us and doubt the very existence of God Himself. He wants us to become weak so he can take over. The enemy comes to steal, kill, and destroy, and that is what he is trying to do with all the gender confusion going on. In June 2023, the California governor signed a bill banning school districts from notifying parents of their child's gender identification or sexual orientation without the child's permission in cases where parents were opposed to the child's gender identification or sexual orientation change (www.npr.org/2024/07/16/nx-s1-5041437/california-bans-school-rules-requiring-parents-notification-of-childs-pronoun-change). And the enemy uses some to divide and conquer us one by one.

The enemy is trying to steal our identities in so many ways: through the definition of family, through racial division, through education, through gender confusion, and even through the church when we replace God's Word and truth with what the world is trying to get us to believe. But Jesus came to give us life and life more abundantly in Him and the identity He gave us while we were in our mothers' wombs.

Do not let the enemy do this to our children or anyone else. We cannot let the enemy divide us. We must stand together. Teach your children through the Word of God who they are and who He created them to be.

Teach your children not to be ashamed of God creating them either a male or a female and to know He had a purpose behind His decision. God did not make a mistake in doing so. Teach them the truth of God's Word and of Jesus Christ so they can know the truth, and the truth shall set them free in Jesus Christ.

In what areas has the enemy tried to attack your identity or the identities of your loved ones? How can you combat those tactics and the lies with the Word of God? How can you stand up for identity truth in this world, your children's schools, or society? How or where may God be calling you to make a stand for His truth?

SOLDIER, ATHLETE, FARMER

You therefore must endure hardship as a good soldier of Jesus Christ. No one engaged in warfare entangles himself with the affairs of this life, that he may please him who enlisted him as a soldier. And also, if anyone competes in athletics, he is not crowned unless he competes according to the rules. The hardworking farmer must be first to partake of the crops. Consider what I say, and may the Lord give you understanding in all things. (2 Timothy 2:3–7 NKJV)

Soldier

First, I have to be a soldier in Christ Jesus and God's kingdom. A soldier has duties, responsibilities, learning, training, and loyalties. Soldiers must learn how to endure hardship. They recognize you cannot be entangled with the affairs of this life. When people come into boot camp, they do not look like soldier material right away, but then transformation occurs. They might not have known they had it in them, and it took drill instructors to help draw out their gifts and soldier abilities and train them to be true soldiers. Or they might know some of what they possess inside and are using it detrimentally, hurting themselves and those around them.

So it takes drill instructors to point them in the right direction. A soldier must learn how to unite with their fellow soldiers. The drill instructor will try to break down soldiers' will to build them up and shift their mindsets to think of their unit as themselves and be able to face combat. God has recruited us into His kingdom and His army, so we must be loyal and committed to the things of God and His kingdom.

Athlete

Athletes usually focus more on their own personal best and push themselves for personal achievement unless they are on a team. The athlete is focused on one goal, winning the prize. The athlete's mindset is that nothing less than victory is good enough. But the athletes usually do so when pushed and have a coach to sharpen skills/talents/gifts. An athlete must endure hours and hours of training to improve, to grow in ability, and to win. Athletes must follow rules for their sports to avoid disqualifications or penalties.

Paul said he fought the good fight, finished the race, and kept the faith. He kept his eye on the true prize of eternal life and blessings from the Lord.

Farmer

A farmer is focused on their family and being able to make money to feed and support them. They also have a sense of responsibility to the community. A farmer must step out in faith to choose to farm. They can sometimes envision the field and crops beforehand. Being a farmer requires vision, hard work, strength, and faith. The farmer must know the seasons and right time of year to plant to produce a good crop. The farmer must cultivate the land, till it, and prepare it to plant the seed. Then the farmer must plant the seed in the ground and nurture the ground to help it grow. After a period of watering and pruning the crops, they will be ready to harvest. So farmers must be focused, faithful, and work hard to produce a large enough crop for their intended uses.

God says His Word is the seed we must plant into the hearts of His harvest of lost souls. We must use wisdom to speak the right words and at the opportune time. God says the harvest is plentiful, but the laborers are few. Let us be the farmers and laborers who go out into God's field and pluck the harvest for His kingdom to bring the lost to know Jesus Christ as their personal Savior and Lord.

Paul gives Timothy these examples of the soldier, athlete, and farmer because they are focused and have a purpose. As members of the kingdom of God, we need some of the same characteristics and attributes in our walk with the Lord. We cannot entangle ourselves with the affairs of the world as we build the kingdom, or we will get distracted and off course. We must stay focused on the prize of the upward call of God in Christ Jesus, like the athlete is focused on winning the prize. And just like the farmer stays busy cultivating the soil, knowing when and what to plant, and how to grow his seed, so must we cultivate our hearts for the seed of God's Word to grow and produce His fruitfulness and characteristics in our lives, hearts, souls, and minds.

What may you need to be let go of to focus on what Christ has called you to do in His kingdom? What areas do you need self-discipline and the training of the Holy Spirit to better reach the prize of the upward call of God in Jesus in your life? What ways do you need to break up the ground in your heart for the seed of God's truth and Word to better produce the fruit of His righteousness and ways in your life?

See 2 Timothy 4:7–8; Luke 8:11; Matthew 9:37.

BELIEVE, STAND, PURSUE

*O*ne day about a year ago, these three words came to me as I was driving to work.

Believe. Believe God's Word and His promises. His promises are yes and Amen in Christ Jesus. His written Word is full of His promises to us. Jesus is the living Word, tried and true. His promises will always line up with His Word; He will never contradict Himself. Believe He is faithful to His promises. Believe God when He says all things are possible with Him. Believe His Word is complete and full of truth. It is alive and brings life to all who obey. Believe God sent His only begotten Son, Jesus, to be born of a virgin, die on the cross for the sins of the world (yours and mine), and rose again on the third day, defeating sin and death for us all to have eternal life with our God and Father in heaven.

Stand. Stand on the promises God has given you. Know He says in His Word that His Word will not return to Him void but will accomplish all that it was sent to do. So stand even when the storms of doubt or unbelief try to rise up, when the storms of life try to take you off course, or when the naysayers try to get you to doubt what God has already said to you. Stand even if the wind tries to knock you down. Stand having done all to stand. Stand on the solid Rock of Jesus Christ, the living, life-giving Word, and stand even more!

Pursue. Pursue the Lord God Almighty and Savior, Jesus Christ. Pursue Him with all your heart and with all your being. Then Jesus will fulfill every promise He has given you and us all. Pursue Jesus, not the promises. Pursue Jesus! Pursue His presence, His face, His character, His grace, His truth, His mercy, His love, and His heart's secrets so we can become more like Him every day and present Jesus Christ to a dying and lost world.

DONNA MCMILLIN

Believe.
Stand.
Pursue.

God's spoken Word to us regarding His written Word, His calling, and His purposes is true and firm. His spoken Word may come through a prophetic word, through something someone says in day-to-day conversation, through a message the pastor preaches, through reading His Word and the scriptures jump out as though God is speaking directly to our hearts, through His presence in worship and prayer as we hear Him whisper in our ears, and even through a prophetic picture or our dreams. God is still speaking to His people. Believe. Stand. Pursue.

> So shall My word be that goes forth from My mouth; it shall not return to Me void, but it shall accomplish what I please, and it shall prosper in the thing for which I sent it. (Isaiah 55:11 NKJV)

> For all the promises of God in Him are Yes, and in Him Amen, to the glory of God through us. (2 Corinthians 1:20 NKJV)

VOICES WE LISTEN TO

*R*efer to section 1 for the accompanying poem, "The Voices We Listen To."

From the day we are born, there are voices speaking into our lives. Scientists say the first five years of a child's life are the most effective for developing the values and character they carry for the rest of their lives. So, it is of great importance we begin speaking God's Word and truth into our children's lives from the time they are in their mothers' wombs. We must speak God's Word and truth, teaching our children their identities in Jesus Christ and developing His character in them. I know there are many things said about positive speaking, and that is good. But positive speaking can only take you so far. Speaking God's Word and teaching the Bible to our children will instill in them the truth that will set them free for life through faith in Jesus Christ.

I can remember all kinds of voices I have listened to my entire life, and not all of them were good. I did not come to know Jesus as my Savior and Lord until I was twenty-four years of age. So until then, many of the things spoken into my life were not His truths and held me in bondage for many years. For example, when I was in the US Marine Corps, a male marine told me if I would lose a little bit of weight and let my hair grow long, I would be more attractive. That was back in the 1982 to 1986 time frame, yet I still remember those words and what they did to me. Thank the Lord Jesus Christ He set me free from those words. External voices come from other people, television, society, classmates, family members, and the world. The voices we listen to and allow into our minds, hearts, and souls can build up or tear down.

But there are also internal voices coming from our own thoughts or the voice of the enemy and the lies he tries to tell us. These can be just as detrimental or effective to us as the outside voices we choose to listen to. I am sure all of us have told ourselves very negative things when we have messed up, gotten bad grades, or just out-and-out did something wrong and hurtful. In the Bible, there are many times when scriptures say someone, "said to themselves." And almost every time that is written, it is not a good thing in the person's life. So we need to be careful in how we speak to ourselves. Words have a way of getting into our minds, spirits, and souls and either tearing down to destroy or building up to life. That old saying, "Sticks and stones may break my bones, but words will never harm me," is not true at all. The minute a false, lying voice speaks to tear you down, take that thought captive to the obedience of Jesus Christ. Tear down every stronghold that tries to say something different than what God says about you in His Word.

When I became a Christian, a child of God, I began to read the Word of God where it tells me who I am in Christ Jesus. I read I am His child, forgiven, washed pure, and given a new life through faith in Jesus Christ. His Word tells me I am His joint heir with God the Father. His Word tells me I am fearfully and wonderfully made in His image! Wow! God's Word of truth sets us free, shows us who we truly are in Him, and builds us up instead of tear us down.

As we go through life, we must be careful about what voices we allow to speak into our hearts. We must be careful about what we watch and listen to. We choose what voices we will listen to; we can decide. The Word of God says that with our words we either speak life or death. His Word brings life; the lies of the devil and of this world bring death. Therefore, choose life from God's Word, and speak it into your life and the lives of your children, family, and those around you. Speak God's Word into your spirit every day to build yourself up in Christ so this world can see what it looks like to be a child of God and recognize it has no hold on you at all.

What voices will you allow into your children's lives and your life? How will you begin to speak about yourself, your children, the people around you? How can you change the way you speak and the voices you listen to? Maybe you can start to listen more to Christian music instead of secular music. Maybe you can read more Christian self-help books and the Bible to know the Word of God and prevent the lies of the enemy from penetrating your heart, mind, soul, or spirit.

> Death and life are in the power of the tongue, and those who love it will eat its fruit. (Proverbs 18:21 NKJV)

For though we walk in the flesh, we do not war according to the flesh. For the weapons of our warfare are not carnal but mighty in God for pulling down strongholds, casting down arguments and every high thing that exalts itself against the knowledge of God, bringing every thought into captivity to the obedience of Christ. (2 Corinthians 10:3–5 NKJV)

Then Jesus said to those Jews who believed Him, "if you abide in My word, you are My disciples indeed. And you shall now the truth, and the truth shall make you free." ... Therefore if the Son makes you free, you shall be free indeed. (John 8:31–32, 36 NKJV)

GOD HAS NOT FORGOTTEN YOU

*R*eading in Matthew 9, I studied the account of Jairus seeking Jesus to heal his daughter who had just died. Mark and John said his daughter was at the point of death when Jairus came seeking Jesus, but it really did not matter because by the time Jesus got to her, she was dead.

And as Jesus was on His way to Jairus's house to heal his daughter, a woman with an issue of blood for twelve years came and touched the hem of Jesus's garment and was healed. The scripture says she said to herself if she could just touch the hem of Jesus's garment, she knew she would be healed.

I have read this scripture many times throughout the years, but this time some interesting and encouraging things stood out to me. Jesus was interrupted on His way to heal Jairus's daughter. Now, Jairus prioritized this task because it was his child who was sick. On their way to his house, someone interrupted them by touching the hem of Jesus's garment and receiving healing. The thing is that Jesus did not treat Jairus's situation as an emergency. He did not worry at all thinking, *Oh no, I have to hurry and get to his daughter.* Jesus stopped right there, turned to the crowd, and asked, "Who touched Me?" The scripture describes this crowd as being shoulder to shoulder, with hardly enough room to move on the street, and they were all there for Jesus to heal them.

Again I say Jesus was on His way to heal or raise up a young girl who was at the point of death. Now to me, that would seem like an emergency. But Jesus knows all things, and He knew who He was and that He would heal both the young girl and the woman with the issue of blood. In fact, I would say Jesus already knew who touched Him, but He wanted to draw her out to confirm her healing. So the woman stepped forward and acknowledged it was her. Jesus told her, her faith had made her well.

After Jesus healed her, then He, Jairus, and the disciples headed to Jairus's house to heal his daughter. Before they arrived, some servants came and told Jairus his daughter was dead so not to bother Jesus. But Jesus stopped Jairus and said, "Only believe." When they got to Jairus's house, many mourners were outside. Jesus told them to be quiet, the girl was only asleep, not dead. They laughed at Jesus because they knew she was dead. So Jesus went inside with a few of His disciples, healed the young girl, and raised her up. All those around were astonished.

Reading again with fresh eyes, I noticed first that Jairus did not panic and try to rush Jesus to his house. Jairus barely spoke up at all, saying only, "Master we must hurry, or my daughter will die." Jairus, too, must have had faith to know no matter what happened, Jesus would heal his daughter.

Second, it came to me that even though Jesus was interrupted and took the time out to heal the woman with issue of blood, He did not forget about Jairus and his daughter. Jairus did not have to remind Jesus. Healing Jairus's daughter was still on Jesus's heart and in His will to do. And Jesus did heal her.

I feel like the Holy Spirit was showing me that we often pray and pray and do not see an immediate answer. It seems other people are getting answers to their prayers as we wait. He revealed for us not to give up hope or get discouraged because Jesus has not forgotten about our prayer requests. Maybe there are some interruptions along the way with others' prayers being answered, but hang in there; wait on the Lord. Jesus has not forgotten about you or your prayers. He is on His way to answer your prayers. Even when it seems like there is no hope, hope in Jesus, the One who hears and answers our prayers in His timing and His way. Trust that Jesus is faithful to His word and promises to us. He hears our prayers, He cares, and He will answer. Tell your soul not to be cast down, but hope in God, our anchor and the lifter of our head. He will strengthen the hearts of those who hope in Him. We continually hope and praise Him in the waiting.

See Matthew 9; Psalms 31:24; 42:5; 71:14; Mark 5; Luke 8; Jeremiah 33:3.

ONE OF THOSE DAYS

> Now it happened on one of those days, as He taught the people in the temple and preached the gospel, that the chief priests and the scribes, together with the elders, confronted Him. (Luke 20:1 NKJV)

This was one of those days. One of those days when religious leaders came to confront Jesus. They wanted to challenge Him and trip Him up in front of all the people, so they could arrest and kill Him. Many religious sects came one right after another to trip Jesus up, but He always came back with a scripture from the Old Testament or a parable and put them in their places. They could not defeat Jesus.

I had to laugh when I read, "Now it happened on one of those days." Have you ever had "one of those days"? Or maybe many of those days or weekends. We all have, and we have all failed at times. But we have not been defeated. I recently had one of those weekends, and I failed miserably. But as I woke up a couple days later, God was there picking me up, patting me on the back, and saying, "Come on now. Get back in the game, and let's go get 'em, champ." He was not leaving me there in my self-pity because of my failure. He offered His mercy again, which is new every morning. He offered His forgiveness immediately and His grace abundantly.

We must choose to receive His mercy, forgiveness, and grace and reach out to take His hand to lift us up again and hear Him say, "Go on, I got this." Jesus has this. Do not let failure keep you down. Confess your sin to God, and receive His forgiveness, mercy, and grace He offers new every day. Even though we may fall seven times a day, He will be there to pick us up, dust us off, and send us on our way. In Jesus, it is a new day every day full of His mercy and grace to start again. Do not let the enemy beat you down. Do not beat yourself up. Run to Jesus, seek and receive His forgiveness and mercy, and get back in the game. And go get 'em, tiger.

Jesus said in John 16:33 (NKJV), "These things I have spoken to you, that in Me you may have peace. In the world you will have tribulation; but be of good cheer, I have overcome the world."

Because Jesus has overcome the world, we have overcome the world and the attacks of the enemy. Though we fall, we are not defeated. He will always pick us back up. Forgive yourself—and forgive others. Know Jesus is our help in and victory over "one of those days."

DONNA MCMILLIN

FAITH, HOPE, AND LOVE: THE GREATEST OF THESE IS LOVE

And she brought forth her firstborn Son, and wrapped Him in swaddling cloths, and laid Him in a manger, because there was no room for them in the inn. Now there were in the same country shepherds living out in the fields, keeping watch over their flock by night. And behold, an angel of the Lord stood before them, and the glory of the Lord shone around them, and they were greatly afraid. Then the angel said to them, "Do not be afraid, for behold, I bring you good tidings of great joy which will be to all people. For there is born to you this day in the city of David a Savior, who is Christ the Lord. And this will be the sign to you: You will find a Babe wrapped in swaddling cloths, lying in a manger." And suddenly there was with the angel a multitude of the heavenly host praising God and saying: "Glory to God in the highest, and on earth peace, goodwill toward men!" So it was, when the angels had gone away from them into heaven, that the shepherds said to one another, "Let us now go to Bethlehem and see this thing that has come to pass, which the Lord has made known to us." And they came with haste and found Mary and Joseph, and the Babe lying in a manger. (Luke 2:7–16 NKJV)

*F*aith—Faith for Mary when the angel appeared to her, announcing she would be the mother of the Christ child, the Son of God. In Luke 1:38 she replied, "Let it be to me according to your word." Faith for the three wise men, who were Gentiles. They had studied the prophecies, saw the signs for the King of the Jews, and then followed the star that led them to the Christ child, the babe Jesus, the King and Savior of the world. Faith for us today in Jesus Christ our Savior and Lord, who is faithful in all His promises and His Word to us.

Hope—Hope when the angels appeared to the shepherds, the lowliest of all occupations at that time, and yet they were the first to hear the good news of a Savior born to us. Hope that flared and stirred inside them and drove them to seek the Babe the angels declared. As the shepherds came face-to-face, such hope overflowed within them to know their God had invited them, considered the lowliest of His people, to look at hope alive in the Babe. Hope for us today as Jesus was for all people, for all mankind.

Love—Love Mary bore in her heart for her baby, the Savior of the world, when she pondered these things in her heart. Love when God gave His only begotten Son for the sins of the world years later on the cross. Love when Jesus hung on that cross, endured humiliation, and suffered such great pain, all for us. Love for all mankind in our Savior Jesus Christ that we, too, now have forgiveness and eternal life.

In our walk with the Lord, we need all three—faith, hope, and love. We must have faith in order to walk with the Lord and in the ways He shows and tells us to go. We must have hope His promises are true, and His ways are the best for us. We must have love for Him and love from Him in order to love others as He loves us. Knowing when we finally see Jesus, either when the rapture happens or in eternity when we take our last breath, faith and hope will no longer be needed because we will be looking into the face of Jesus, who is our faith and hope. But love will always be with us because God is love, and we must have love for all eternity.

As you look at faith, hope, and love, which do you believe you may be lacking more of? Do you agree that of these three, love is the most important? How can we love the Lord better and love others better like He loves us and others?

A love that says all things are possible
And proves that is God's principle.

A love so powerful it casts out all fear
And says to doubt you are no longer welcomed here.

A love that silences all insecurity
And says in Jesus is our identity.

A love that covers all our sins and wrongs,
A love that rejoices over us with songs.

A love that conquered death and hell,
A love that says, "Oh my soul, now all is well."

> Faith, hope, and love, but the greatest of these is love ... love
> of a Heavenly Father and Jesus our Savior to redeem us back
> to God and be Emmanuel God with us ... Jesus!
>
> And now abide faith, hope, love, these three; but the greatest
> of these is love. (1 Corinthians 13:13 NKJV)

CONSIDER YOUR DESTINY: THOUGHTS ON APRIL 11, 2022

Her uncleanness is in her skirts; she did not consider her destiny; therefore her collapse was awesome; she had no comforter. "O Lord, behold my affliction, for the enemy is exalted!" (Lamentations 1:9 NKJV)

"*S*he did not consider her destiny."

This statement in Lamentations 1:9 stood out to me. Israel had sinned; they began to worship idols and not the true living God of their fathers Abraham, Isaac, and Jacob. And in their disobedience to all the ways that God had instructed them to live, they did not consider the destiny or purposes and plans God had for them.

Likewise, when we choose to sin against God and disobey His Word concerning our lives, we are not considering our destiny in Jesus and the kingdom of God. The Bible says sin is pleasurable for a moment, but it brings death. And if we are just thinking of the pleasure sin can bring, it is easy to forget or overlook the purposes and plans of our God for our lives. Do not let the pleasure of sin deceive you. Ask the Lord to help you keep your eyes on the destiny, purpose, and plans He has for your life. Consequently, when you are tempted to sin, you will discern how it deviates from God's good plans for you. And instead, you can choose to be obedient to the Lord and consider your destiny in Him.

Choose to walk in the instruction of the Word of God, which leads us to our destiny in Him and leads us to life and life more abundantly and His blessings in Jesus Christ.

Prayer

Father, help us to continually keep our destiny in You and Your kingdom in our thoughts and hearts. Keep us from the temptation to walk in our own ways and from sins that lead us away from You. Give us discernment and wisdom. Keep us spiritually awake, alert, and sober-minded daily, and dress us with Your full armor to help us to withstand and overcome the schemes, traps, lies, and nets of the enemy. Lord, we want Your destiny, purposes, and plans for our lives that lead to life and life abundant. Daily, we desire to draw closer to You to personally know Your ways and Your heart and Your presence in our lives. Fill us, Holy Spirit, and we will overflow with Your rivers of living water and choose You! In Jesus's name, Amen!

I'D RATHER HAVE JESUS THAN ANYTHING: THOUGHTS ON MAY 17, 2022

Reading from the gospel of Mark today, where Jesus told His disciples to follow Him, they would have to deny themselves and pick up their crosses. Peter told Jesus they gave up everything for Him, and Jesus responded that whoever gives up everything for Him will have even more in this lifetime and in eternal life. John the Baptist said he must decrease and Jesus must increase in him. Even in Galatians, the Word of God says it is Christ who lives in me, not myself anymore.

And even thinking about Abraham, how God asked Abraham to sacrifice his only son, Isaac. Abraham was obedient to the fullest. Just as he was about to bring the knife down on Isaac, an angel of the Lord stopped him, and God knew right then that Abraham would be willing to give up anything for Him. God provided an offering at that time for Abraham, as God has provided a sacrificial offering for us in Jesus Christ, His only Son, when He died on the cross for us.

My prayer is if there are things in my life the Lord is asking me to surrender to Him, they die in me so He may live bigger in me. Is there anything He would ask me to give up that I might not be willing to give up for Him? Maybe He will not even require me to give it up but is confirming I am willing to release it if He asks. Because if I am not willing, it may be a stronghold in my life that I need to remove.

Do we have the courage to ask Jesus, "Do I need to give this or that up? Is there anything in my life I need to surrender to You and let go of?" Is there a relationship that you need to let go of? What about drinking alcohol? Yes, you may not get drunk, but does the Lord want you to give it up? Is He OK with that in your life? Are we willing to give up anything for Jesus if He asks us?

I would rather have Jesus than anything, as the old song goes. And what He gives in return is a hundred times better for me than anything I could hold on to on my own. So let it go. Let the Lord have control. Surrender it to the Lord! Whatever it is He may ask, it is well worth it!

See Mark 8; John 3:30; Galatians 2:20; Genesis 22.

ARE WE LOVING GOD WITH ALL OUR HEART, SOUL, AND MIND?

Jesus said to him, "You shall love the Lord your God with all your heart, with all your soul, and with all your mind." (Matthew 22:37 NKJV)

Serve the Lord with all your heart. (1 Samuel 12:20 NKJV)

Heart: *Strong's* #3820—knowledge, soul, resolution, determination, conscience, thinking, reflection, inclination, seat of emotions and passions, seat of courage, seat of appetites

Love: *Strong's* #25—take pleasure in, long for

All: *Strong's* #3650—the whole, entire, complete

Soul: *Strong's* #5590 —breath, spirit, abstractly, concretely

Mind: *Strong's* #1271—deep thought, properly, the faculty, by implication, its exercise

*J*esus commanded us to love the Lord our God with all our heart, soul, and mind. Are we truly loving Him with all our heart? Have we given Him our whole heart to be able to love fully? Are we holding back any aspect of our hearts from our God and Savior Jesus Christ? Do our words or actions say to the Lord, "OK, Lord, You can have this, this, and this area of our hearts, but not that area of our hearts"? Do we put our love for our children or spouse above our love for God? God is the keeper of our hearts. We can entrust Him with our entire heart. The Lord will not hurt or damage our hearts. In fact, He will do the opposite. He mends the brokenhearted. He will never trample on our hearts like man can. God desires our hearts to be His in every aspect. He loves us beyond measure. He proved it by sending

His One and only Son, Jesus Christ, to die on the cross for our sins and pay the price we could not. He is a good and great heavenly Father.

God's Word calls us to seek Him, love Him, serve Him, trust Him, turn to Him, and believe in Him with all our heart. God searches our hearts (Jeremiah 17:10). God knows the secrets of our hearts (Psalm 44:21) already, so why not give Him our whole heart. The psalmist said in Psalm 28:7 that his heart trusted in the Lord, and he was helped. Therefore, his heart greatly rejoiced. God knows how to tend to our hearts. He is the gardener of our hearts. He plucks out the weeds that get in and try to choke our hearts from believing, loving, serving, seeking, trusting, and turning to Him completely. Then He plants more seeds of faith and love, empowering us to believe, seek, love, serve, trust, and turn to Him with all our hearts. God desires our entire heart, and if we hold back any part, we will not experience His fullness or His great love as wholly as He desires us to.

In 2 Chronicles 25:2, it says King Amaziah (king of Judah) did what was right in the sight of the Lord but not with a loyal heart. Amaziah's heart was divided. He did not give his entire or complete heart and devotion to the Lord; this can be seen in verses 14–24. Loyal means to give or show firm and constant support or allegiance to a person or institution. So in this case, Amaziah did not give or show firm support without wavering. When he defeated the Edomites, he took their idols and set them up as gods in his house. He was not totally devoted to the Lord God Almighty.

Today, can we do as the psalmist did in Psalm 139:23 and ask God to search us, know our hearts, try us, and reveal our anxieties and the aspects of our hearts we are withholding. We can then fully surrender our whole hearts to our God who loves us with His whole heart and entire being. He has held nothing back from us. He freely gave all of His heart to us. Let us surrender our whole hearts to Him and trust Him to mend our broken hearts. God is the strength of our heart and our portion forever (Psalm 73:26).

Lord, help us release our whole hearts to You. We surrender completely to You, trusting You to mend and keep our hearts in Your love and mercy. Protect our hearts from harm, bitterness, unforgiveness, or anything that is not of You. And cleanse our hearts so they are made whole in Jesus Christ. Holy Spirit, help us to not hold back any aspect of our hearts so we can experience the fullness of what it means to love, serve, seek, believe, trust, and turn to You with our whole hearts. Help us to be men and women after Your own heart. In Jesus's name, Amen!

See Psalm 44:21; 139:23; 73:26; 28:7; Jeremiah 29:13; 17:10; Proverbs 3:5; Joel 2:12; Acts 8:37; 1 Samuel 12:20, 24; Matthew 22:37.

Definitions are found on www.dictionary.com.

DONNA MCMILLIN

THE AMAZINGNESS OF GOD

*Y*ou know what is totally and truly amazing, wonderful, and powerful? The fact our heavenly Father—God of all creation, God who created the heavens and the earth and the glorious expanse of the universe—hears us all when we pray. Get that: He hears our prayers and answers them. Now get this. When we pray, billions of others across the world are praying at the same time, but our all-knowing, all-powerful, ever-present God hears each of our voices individually praying to Him as if we were the only ones praying to Him at that time. He hears each voice lifted to Him because He knows each of us by name. He named every star and galaxy, and He knows each of us by name! Not only that, He also knows our every thought before we even think it. He knew us before we were even formed in our mothers' wombs, and He wrote our names down with a purpose in mind. We are fearfully and wonderfully made. We are His workmanship, His masterpiece. He even knows the numbers of hairs on our heads. I know for some of you that is not much because you do not have any hair on your head, but for some, you have a ton of hairs on your heads, and He knows the number.

And most of all, His thoughts toward us are frequent and numerous, so numerous they cannot be counted. It would be like the sands of the sea. We cannot possibly count the number of times our heavenly Father, God of all creation, thinks about us. And as if that was not enough, He loves us so, so, so greatly that He sent His only begotten Son, Jesus Christ, to die on the cross for our sins and rise again on the third day. Jesus defeated death and sin for us once and for all because we could not pay that price. And through faith in Jesus, His death and resurrection over sin/death, we have eternal life with our heavenly Father. We experience Jesus's righteousness through His blood shed for us on the cross, cleansing us and purifying us so that through faith in Jesus Christ, we can have right standing with God, be forgiven for our sins, and be called His son/daughter.

God did all this with Jesus even while we were enemies with Him.

He did it anyway because His love for us was so great. He is a holy and righteous God, and sin cannot abide in His presence. Therefore, He made the sacrifice and substituted Jesus Christ to die once and for all on the cross for all mankind.

This is totally and truly amazing grace and abundant love. I pray you hear the voice of God today, calling you and telling you how much He loves you. I pray you will call out to Jesus and admit to Him you are a sinner (just like I did) and need His forgiveness and cleansing. Ask Him to forgive you and come into your heart. Then receive and believe in Him as Savior. Let Jesus be Lord over every area of your life. Surrender so that it is no longer you who live but Christ living in you.

See Psalms 40:5; 139:1–10, 12–18, 23–24; 147:4–5; Isaiah 49:5; Jeremiah 29:11; Psalm 94:11; Matthew 10:30; John 10:27–28; Psalm 17:8; John 16:23; Jeremiah 33:3; John 15:16; 2 Chronicles 7:14; Psalm 55:17; John 3:16; Romans 3:23; 5:8; 6:23; 10:9–10, 13; Acts 2:21–39; 4:12; John 14:6; 2 Corinthians 5:17; Ephesians 2:8–9; 4:21–24.

GOD HEARS OUR CRIES

I thought this appropriate to share on our anniversary today. It was written several years ago.

About fifteen or sixteen years ago, my husband was working out of town, and I went to spend the week with him. One night I had a dream. Sometimes the Lord would give me dreams, and this was definitely one of those times. In my dream, my pastor told me, "Donna, read 1 Samuel 1:1–8, and read it out loud. There is something about saying the Word of God aloud." And in my dream, I started reading it aloud. Then I woke up.

I grabbed my Bible and started reading 1 Samuel 1:1–8 aloud. Well, in a whisper so I didn't wake up my husband. This scripture is about Hannah, a woman who struggled to conceive and endured the taunting of her husband's other wife because she was barren. In verse 8, Hannah's husband asks, "Am I not better to you than ten sons?" This verse stood out to me. And I understood the Lord to say that even though we could not have children, He would be better to me than ten sons. Also, He promised Jim would be better to me than ten sons. God has truly been faithful in this promise He gave to me. Both the Lord and my husband have been better to me than ten sons could have been. God never fails! Love never fails!

My husband and I were never able to have children, and it broke my heart. I had two ectopic pregnancies in my first marriage and lost one of my fallopian tubes when it burst during my second pregnancy. When I saw young women having children out of wedlock, it would cause me to question the Lord. I could rejoice with women getting pregnant; I really could. But a part of me was hurting at those times. Through the years I had cried out to the Lord many times. I remember one day sobbing my eyes out.

Then one day I came into church and was going about my usher duties. And it just hit me. I surrendered it all to the Lord. I simply said, "Lord, I trust that You know best. You give Your best to Your children, and You have and will continue to give Your best to me and my husband, so I trust You even in this hurt." And He has mended my heart. God knows everything, and He sees the big picture. He knows what is best for us, and I trust Him to give me His best always.

In life, things do not always go as we plan or as we would like. It does not mean God has abandoned us or forgotten us in any way. God hears every cry of our hearts, and we can trust in His plans because He knows what is best for us. We can trust in His love for us because He has shown us the depths of His love in dying on the cross to give us eternal life through faith in Jesus Christ. We must come to a point where we just lay it all down and trust that our all-knowing, all-loving, and merciful God and Savior, Jesus Christ's will and way are better than anything we could ever think of for our own lives.

Do you feel like God has forgotten about promises He made to you? Do you feel like your plans for your life are not going the way you thought they should? Are there areas in your life where you need to truly surrender to the Lord? Areas that cause you pain and make you feel forgotten? Turn to the Lord God Almighty, and trust Him to work all things out for your good and His glory.

> There was a certain man of Ramathaim-Sophia, of the hill country of Ephraim, named Elkanah the son of Jeroham, the son of Elihu, the son of Thou, the son of Zuph, and Ephraimite. He had two wives, one named Hannah and the other named Peninnah. Peninnah had children, but Hannah had none. This man went up from his city each year to worship and sacrifice to the Lord of hosts at Shiloh. Hophni and Phinehas, the two sons of Eli, were priests to the Lord there. When the day came that Elkanah sacrificed, he would give portions [of the sacrificial meat] to Peninnah his wife and all her sons and daughters. But to Hannah he would give a double portion because he loved Hannah, but the Lord had given her no children. Hannah's rival provoked her bitterly, to irritate and embarrass her, because the Lord had left her childless. So, it happened year after year, whenever she went up to the house of the Lord Peninnah provoked her; so she wept and would not eat. Then Elkanah her husband said to her, "Hannah, why do you cry and why do you not eat? Why are you so sad and discontent? Am I not better to you than ten sons?" (1 Samuel 1:1–8 AMP)

LOVE OF CHRIST COMPELS US

> For the love of Christ compels us, because we judge thus: that if One died for all, then all died; and He died for all, that those who live should live no longer for themselves, but for Him who died for them and rose again. Therefore, from now on, we regard no one according to the flesh. Even though we have known Christ according to the flesh, yet now we know Him thus no longer. Therefore, if anyone is in Christ, he is a new creation; old things have passed away; behold, all things have become new. Now all things are of God, who has reconciled us to Himself through Jesus Christ, and has given us the ministry of reconciliation, that is, that God was in Christ reconciling the world to Himself, not imputing their trespasses to them, and has committed to us the word of reconciliation. Now the, we are ambassadors for Christ, as though God were pleading through us: we implore you on Christ's behalf, be reconciled to God. For He made Him who knew no sin to be sin for us, that we might become the righteousness of God in Him. (2 Corinthians 5:14–21)

The love of Christ compels us even in our faith because by faith, we know and believe that Jesus died for us and rose again. His great love for us drives us to want to die to ourselves and live for Him when we realize He suffered and died for us on the cross so that we can live forever. As we grasp the depth of His love, we want to live for Him and according to His will. We cannot do anything else but love the Lord and walk in ways pleasing to Him because He loved us first and proved it on the cross. Who would do that for us? Only Jesus Christ, who was sinless and holy, was able to make the ultimate sacrifice for us by laying down His life so that we may live. That is the kind of love that compels us!

The love of Christ Jesus compels us to regard no one in the flesh again. Jesus walked on the earth for thirty-three years but died and rose again with a new body, a resurrected body. So when a person is born again, they become a new creation in Christ Jesus, and the old man is passed away along with his old ways of sin. All things become new in that person and their lives. They are transformed by the love of Jesus, and their minds are renewed by the Word of God. So we are not to look at people and see their old lives or sins. We are to see them in their new state of being born again. We need to ask the Lord to help us see people as He sees them, especially our brothers and sisters in Christ. First Peter 4:8 says, "And above all things have fervent love for one another, for love will cover a multitude of sins." I think of fervent love the same as the "love" Paul uses in 2 Corinthians 5:14 because fervent love will compel us to look at others through the eyes of the Lord Jesus.

The love of Christ compels us to be reconcilers. Jesus has given us the ministry of reconciliation to help reconcile people to God through faith in Jesus Christ. We are ambassadors of Christ, so we are to represent and imitate Him in our lives, pointing people to His love and restoring right relationships with God the Father through faith in Jesus, His Son. Our lives become a witness of the love and power of God. Therefore, we pray for the lost, but we also live our lives as examples and invite others to know the love of Christ that compels them to turn from everything else and completely to Jesus.

Is there any area of your life that the love of Christ needs to compel you to be different? To love differently? To walk differently? To look at people as Jesus does?

FOLLOW ME: JOHN 21:15-22

$\mathcal{K}$nowing that Jesus had risen, Peter and the disciples decided to return to fishing, their occupation prior to following Him. Maybe it was a way for Peter to reflect on what had happened, how he denied Jesus three times, or to try to calm himself with something familiar. They fished all night and caught nothing. Then the next morning, Jesus called to them from the shore, asking if they caught any food. They answered no. Then Jesus told them to throw their net on the right side of the boat. Jesus knows how to provide for His children and guides us to our needs. But Jesus also cared for them even though they went back to something familiar. So they threw the net on the right side and caught so many fish they struggled to draw it back in.

Then, John recognized it was Jesus and told Peter. Peter took off his outer garment and jumped into the water to swim to the shore while the others rowed the boat to shore. Jesus had a fire going, and they cooked and ate. This was the third time Jesus showed Himself to His disciples.

After eating, Jesus pulled Peter to the side and talked to him privately. Now, Peter had denied Jesus three times, and each time Jesus asked Peter, "Do you love Me?" I believe Jesus did so to really sow in Peter that he was forgiven and to help him see God's love and purpose for his life.

Three times Jesus asked Peter if he loved Him. The first time He asked him if he loved Jesus more than the other disciples. Peter responded, "Yes, Lord. You know that I love You." Jesus responded, "Feed My lambs." The second time Jesus asked Peter if he loved Him, Peter responded the same as the first time, and Jesus said, "Tend My sheep." Both the first and second times Jesus asked Peter if he loved Him, Jesus was using the agape word for love, meaning the complete, unconditional love of God above all else. But Peter did not understand and answered Jesus with the phileo type of love (Peter's brotherly love for Jesus). So the third time Jesus asked Peter if he loved Him, Jesus used phileo because that was all Peter could understand and give at the moment. Peter was grieved that Jesus asked him a third time but responded the same as before. Jesus told Peter to feed His sheep and even began to tell Peter what type of death he would glorify God with at the end of his life.

All three times Jesus was reiterating God's calling on Peter's life. Then Jesus said, "Follow Me." I believe Jesus was reminding Peter to keep his eyes on Him, not to look at circumstances or the sufferings he would go through for the name of Jesus, and not to get distracted by others.

Because Peter turned and saw John following them, Peter asked Jesus, "What about this man?" Jesus basically answered, "What is it to you, Peter, what I have in store for John. You just follow Me, Peter, and don't worry about him." I believe the Lord is showing us that each of us has a different calling and different gifts God personally assigned to us, and we cannot compare ourselves to others. We cannot watch whether someone else is doing what they are supposed to be doing because we have no control over them.

Our only responsibility is to busy ourselves doing what God has called us to do—follow Jesus! As we follow Jesus, our eyes are forward; if we turn around to look at others, we lose sight of Jesus and where He is leading us. We must keep our eyes on Jesus to follow Him, not on man or anything else. Do not worry about what others are or are not doing. Just focus on and walk in the calling God has put on you. When you do that, you will be like Peter as he walked faithfully in his calling, tending Jesus's sheep until the end of his days, glorifying the Lord then and even in his death.

DONNA MCMILLIN

THE RENEWING OF OUR MINDS

*W*hen Adam and Eve were created, before they fell and sin crept in, their thought processes were in the image of God. Their minds were right with God as they walked with Him in the garden. But when Adam and Eve were tempted and gave in to sin, their minds were invaded by the corruption of sin. That is why Romans 12:2 says we are to be transformed by the "renewing" of our minds. Our minds were new before sin, pure before sin, but then our minds became corrupt or impure, and we were no longer in our right frame of mind—the mind and image of God. So our minds must be renewed.

Renew means to begin or take up again; to restore or replenish; to make, say, or do again; to revive; to recover; to restore to a former state.

God must transform us by renewing our minds, so our thought process is restored to its state before sin. Now, how does God do that? He imparts His Word in us and utilizes the transforming power of the Holy Spirit. Transform means to change in form, appearance of structure; to change in condition, nature, or character, convert. Transformation is a heart change that also causes changes to the way we think and see circumstances.

Conform means to make similar in form, nature, or character; to act in accordance with. There is no real change from the inside out. Brainwashing, a method of systematically changing attitudes or altering beliefs, originated in totalitarian counties, especially through the use of drugs, torture, or physiological stress techniques, any method of controlled systematic indoctrination, especially based on repetition or confusion. Neither of these cause a heart change, just an outward change or a total indoctrination of one's own way of thinking for themselves.

If we abide (live, dwell, soak up, read) in His Word, we will know the truth of God, and the truth will set us free, the truth that transforms by renewing our minds from a sin nature back to God's way and righteousness. Our minds must be restored to their former state in the garden of Eden. Sin leads us farther and farther way from God's original design for us, causing confusion and corruption in our thoughts and way of thinking. Sin deceives us, causing our thoughts and minds to stray from God's truth and ways. His Word renews even our process of thinking.

The Word of God is truth, and our minds must be renewed by truth in order to take captive every thought in obedience to Jesus Christ (2 Corinthians 10:5). Jesus said in John 8:31, "If you abide in My word, you are My disciples indeed. And you shall know the truth, and the truth shall make you free." And verse 36 says, "Therefore if the Son makes you free, you shall be free indeed."

Going back to 2 Corinthians 10:3–5, it says that although we may walk on this earth with a fleshly body, we do not war according to the flesh. Our weapons are not carnal (of this world, like spears, swords, guns, and so on). Our weapons are mighty in God for tearing down strongholds and casting down arguments and high things that try to exalt themselves against the knowledge of God, bringing every thought captive to the obedience of Jesus Christ. One of the weapons of our warfare is the Word of God, which is truth that cannot be dismantled. So when a thought comes into our minds by the power of the Holy Spirit and His Word in our hearts (knowing His Word because we have read His Word), we can dissect each thought to see if it lines up with the Word of God. His Word can set us free of any thought that is not of God.

But we cannot take every thought captive and be set free unless we know the truth from reading and abiding in His Word, the Bible. God wants to transform us back to His image of holiness and righteousness through faith in Jesus Christ, and He does it by renewing our minds with His truth, His Word. He restores our minds to the way He created them to think on things that are true, noble, just, pure, lovely, of a good report, virtuous, and praiseworthy. Many psalms tell us to meditate on God's Word, His precepts, on Jesus, on His awesome works, His truth, and on who He is, which aids in our renewal and freedom.

God's renewing takes us back to our original state of thinking, before sin entered our hearts and minds. Brainwashing strips us of our ability to think in order to get us to think the way someone else wants us to think. Doing so brings us closer to God's heart and love so we can know Him and His Son, Jesus Christ, with the indwelling of His Holy Spirit living in us in a deeper and intimate way. We can then spend eternity with God in a new heaven and new earth.

Sometimes we allow tradition, culture, and education to tell us how we are to think. But God wants to renew our minds back to His original design. Are there ways from your tradition or culture that fall short of or contradict God's truth? How can you allow God's Word to renew your mind and thinking? How can you combat the lies the enemy tries to use in your life to guide your thinking? What thoughts and ways do you need to lay down and let God completely change the way you think?

> I beseech you therefore, brethren, by the mercies of God, that you present your bodies a living sacrifice, holy, acceptable to God, which is your reasonable service. And do not be conformed to this world, but be transformed by the renewing of your mind, that you may prove what is that good and acceptable and perfect will of God. (Romans 12:1–2 NKJV)

> For though we walk in the flesh, we do not war according to the flesh. For the weapons of our warfare are not carnal but mighty in God for pulling down strongholds, casting down arguments and every high thing that exalts itself against the knowledge of God, bringing every thought into captivity to the obedience of Christ, and being ready to punish all disobedience when your obedience is fulfilled. (2 Corinthians 10:3–6 NKJV)

> Then Jesus said to those Jews who believed Him, "If you abide in My word, you are My disciples indeed. And you shall know the truth, and the truth shall make you free." … Jesus answered them, "Most assuredly, I say to you, whoever commits sin is a slave of sin. And a slave does not abide in the house forever, but a son abides forever. Therefore if the Son makes you free, you shall be free indeed." (John 8:31–32, 34–36 NKJV)

> Finally, brethren, whatever things are true, whatever things are noble, whatever things are just, whatever things are pure, whatever things are lovely, whatever things are of good report, if there is any virtue and if there is anything praiseworthy— meditate on these things. (Philippians 4:8 NKJV)

Definitions are found on www.dictionary.com.

CHOOSE GOD'S WAY

Our ways are not always God's ways. And if our truth or ways are contradictory to the Word of God, they are wrong. God's ways are higher than our ways. We may not always understand His ways, but we can trust that He loves us beyond measure and has only our best in mind as we read His Word and obey His truth. God's truth, the Bible, is truth period. And we can only know His ways, His truth, and His Word as we begin to read and study His Word. We cannot know what His ways are or how we are to live unless we are constantly in His Word and in His presence, being filled and led by the Holy Spirit. How will we know how to live a life pleasing to the Lord God Almighty if we do not know His truth, His Word, or His ways? We must abide in His Word, and allow Jesus, God's living Word, to abide in us, and let the Holy Spirit rule and reign in our lives completely. His Word is from everlasting to everlasting and is the Rock (Jesus) on which we can stand forever. His Word is immovable and powerful. His Word is healing and saves to the uttermost, transforms us as we read it daily, and renews our minds so that His ways become our ways, and His truth becomes our truth.

When we deviate from the ways and Word of God and living a life pleasing to Him, the enemy comes to steal, kill, and destroy the works of God in our lives. Jesus came to give us life and life abundantly, and that life is found only in Him as Savior and Lord of our lives.

Jesus is the only way to God. Jesus is the truth, the way, the life. No one can come to God the Father but through faith in Jesus! Jesus said in John 8:31–32 that if we abide in His Word, we are His disciples indeed. We shall know the truth, and the truth shall set us free. Verse 36 says the Son—Jesus—makes us free.

No matter how personal or close we get to the things the world calls good but the Lord calls sin, we should never compromise on the truth of God's Word. His ways, His truths are the truth, and His love is absolute. His love accepts us as we are but loves us enough to cleanse and save us through the blood of Jesus. It transforms us through the reading of God's Word and the living Word (Jesus). It renews our minds with His truth. When perversions of truth show up close to home, maybe God is causing us to become more compassionate and loving without compromising His truth. God's ways are higher than our ways, and Jesus had to give His life to pay the price for our sins and the sins of the world.

I will honor His sacrifice and stand on His Word and truth filled with His love and the Holy Spirit. I will walk in compassion and in a love that draws people away from the sin that destroys them and helps lead them to repentance before a loving and living God.

> We can make our own plans, but the Lord gives the right answer. People may be pure in their own eyes, but the Lord examines their motives. Commit your actions to the Lord, and your plans will succeed. Unfailing love and faithfulness make atonement for sin. By fearing the Lord, people avoid evil. When people's lives please the Lord, even their enemies are at peace with them. We can make our plans, but the Lord determines our steps. Those who listen to instruction will prosper; those who trust the Lord will be joyful. There is a path before each person that seems right, but it ends in death. (Proverbs 16:1–3, 6–7, 9, 20, 25 NLT)

> People ruin their lives by their own foolishness and then are angry at the Lord. Keep the commandments and keep your life; despising them leads to death. You can make many plans, but the Lord's purpose will prevail. Fear of the Lord leads to life, bringing security and protection from harm. (Proverbs 19:3, 16, 21, 23 NLT)

PUSHING THROUGH, SIDE BY SIDE

$\mathcal{J}$ was reading in Nehemiah one morning. Nehemiah heard how his people and Jerusalem were doing, and he wept, he prayed, and he sought God for favor and answers. God answered his prayers and gave him favor with the king, allowing him to go to Jerusalem and rebuild the walls of the city.

Then he went to Jerusalem to see the city and destruction for himself. He went out alone for a moment, and God gave him a strategy to rebuild the wall because God was still with His people.

The people responded. I loved the passage that detailed, by name, each person and group who helped rebuild side by side with the repeated phrase, "next to them ... built." There was even a perfumer to help rebuild the wall around the city. Everyone took their places. Even if they were not exactly gifted to build, they stood next to their fellow man and pitched in. They stood side by side; there was not a place on that wall that did not have someone there rebuilding. Yes, there were the naysayers, but focus was not on the naysayers. They believed God and continued to rebuild the walls around the city. They stood side by side doing the work of the Lord. They did not let fear guide them. They had each other's backs, protecting each other on the wall from the enemy.

And when naysayers threatened to attack, God gave Nehemiah a strategy, a plan to keep building the wall and to fight at the same time. The people took up a tool to rebuild in one hand and took up a sword to fight and protect in the other hand. They put watchmen around; Nehemiah told the people if something were to come up, they would blow the trumpet to alert everyone so they would know when to fight.

God thwarted the plans of the enemy, who tried to come against and put fear in the people of God. God thwarted the enemy's plans because Nehemiah, the leader, sought the Lord, heard the plans of the Lord, and trusted the Lord. The builders stood their ground. They did not run. They did not let fear grip them. They trusted that the Lord their God was with them, and they rebuilt and were prepared to fight at the same time. That is a word for us today: to rebuild and fight at the same time! Stand, trust, rebuild, and fight simultaneously for the Lord our God is with us, and He will thwart the plans of the enemy in this day too. Stand together with our Christian brothers and sisters, side by side, building together, and having each other's back. God has our backs, and He is fighting for us. So stand and see that the battle is the Lord's, and He fights for His children. And we are victorious in Him.

CLEANSING OF TOXINS

A few years back, my body broke out in a rash, similar in appearance to measles, from head to toe. It was extremely painful and itchy twenty-four seven, keeping me awake most nights. I went to a holistic medical doctor, and he prescribed a spray to remove toxins from my body. One day while using the spray, I was out running and began thinking about the fact I was using something that is pushing toxins out of my body, but if I kept eating toxic foods (sweets and bad carbs), I was being counterproductive. For the spray to produce the necessary results and cleanse my body of toxins, it was imperative that I was not allowing toxic food into my body during this time.

I felt like the Holy Spirit said the same is true in our spiritual lives. The Holy Spirit dwells within us, and His role is to push the toxins of the old man, the toxins of the world, and the toxins of the flesh out of us. The Holy Spirit rids us of the works of the flesh (adultery, fornication, uncleanness, lewdness, idolatry, sorcery, hatred, contentions, jealousies, outbursts of wrath, selfish ambitions, divisions, heresies, envy, murders, drunkenness, revelries and the likes) and cleanses us so we can produce the fruit of the Spirit (love, joy, peace, long-suffering, kindness, goodness, faithfulness, gentleness, and self-control (Galatians 5:19–23). Toxins are sins—evil, darkness, wickedness, injustice, and unrighteousness. The problem comes when we allow sin back in through toxic things we watch, read, or listen to and allow into our hearts, spirits, souls, or minds. Such behavior is counterproductive to what the Holy Spirit is doing in our lives. So as the Holy Spirit asked me, I ask you, what toxins are we still allowing in that are polluting our souls, minds, hearts, and spirits?

We have to purposely choose to break agreement with all the old toxic thought patterns, mindsets, and sins we try to hang on to and allow the Holy Spirit to cleanse us and change us every single minute of the day. We must surrender control to Him, and He will transform us, making us more like Jesus every day. Again, we must ask what toxic things we invited in that contradicts the Word of God and cause us to not be imitators of Jesus Christ. Galatians 5:24 says those who are Christ's have crucified the flesh with its passions and desires. Let us give full rein to the Holy Spirit to crucify our flesh with its passions and desires and bring to life God's great passions and desires in every aspect of our beings. Let us give the Holy Spirit full rein to push out every toxin that keeps us from imitating our Lord and Savior Jesus Christ.

Prayer

> Holy Spirit, open our eyes to see any toxins that pollute our souls, minds, spirits, hearts, and lives that we may not have surrendered to You or that we may still be letting in through all we surround ourselves with. Lord, let us be willing to lay it down and submit to Your cleansing and transformative power through the Holy Spirit. Make us into the new man in Christ Jesus and help us lay down all our old ways before You came into our lives. Have Your way, Holy Spirit. Move in a mighty way so our minds have Your thoughts, and Your ways prevail in and through us. Help us to grow every day in the newness of the image of Jesus Christ from the inside out. In Jesus's name, Amen!

THE IMPACT OF OUR PRAYERS

*I*n 2 Chronicles 6, Solomon began to pray after he finished building the temple for the Lord God to dwell. He blessed the people and then blessed the Lord. Finally, he dedicated the house of the Lord. Then Solomon began praying for God to hear the prayers of the people of Israel and forgive them of various sins if they returned to this temple and repented.

In 2 Chronicles 7, God responded to King Solomon's prayer in verse 6, first by fire coming down from heaven and consuming the sacrifices Israel offered and then by His glory filling the temple. In chapter 7, verse 12, God told Solomon He heard his prayers and responded with verse 14: "if My people who are called by My name humble will themselves, and pray and seek My face and turn from their wicked ways, then I will hear from heaven, will forgive their sin and will heal their land." And in verse 15, God says He will see and hear all prayers offered in the house of the Lord. If you read the Bible, you will see God did exactly as He said by hearing Israel's prayers of repentance and forgiving them generation after generation, even in our times now!

Wow, the impact of our prayers!

God hears and responds to our prayers and cries to Him. Meditate on that for a minute. God our Creator hears and responds to our prayers. What an impact our prayers must make to enter the ears of our God and create a response from Him. God loves to hear His people cry out to Him. Just think, we are still praying the response from God to Solomon's prayer found in 2 Chronicles 7:14!

What responses from God to your prayers will your children and grandchildren still be praying to the Lord for generations to come?

What impact will our payers have on future generations?

Keep praying and crying out to the Lord for our loved ones, our nations, our governmental leaders, the church, and this world to see the impact of how God responds to our prayers, especially those where we humble ourselves and pray and seek His face and turn from our wicked ways.

DONNA MCMILLIN

DADDY GOD

Our Daddy God

When I was in high school, I did not know the Lord Jesus Christ as my Savior and Lord. I worked at McDonald's, and one night as I was closing, I asked my daddy about going to a party. He said no. I went to the party anyway. I was walking in disobedience to my father with alcohol involved. Then suddenly, someone said, "Hey, here comes someone's dad." I got up, knowing it was my daddy, and headed to the door. I opened the door, and sure enough, there was my daddy coming to get me.

You see, I was not safely at home with my daddy, so he came looking for me. He did not know exactly where I was, but he searched me out and found me to bring me home where I belonged. That is what our Daddy God does to each of us. Our true home is with Daddy God, and He searches for us and comes to where we are to get us. He brings us back home to dwell in His arms of safety, love, and protection.

No matter where you are in your life, God will come looking for you to draw you back to Him, to your original place of dwelling, where He meant for you to be. He returns you to His presence to live with Him for all eternity.

Daddy God,

I thank You that You are a loving Father who desires us to be with You forever. I praise You. Your love is unfailing and never-ending toward us. I praise You because You showed us how much You loved us on the cross, dying for our sins so we can have a restored relationship with You through the blood of Jesus. I thank You for coming to look for us. Even into our deepest pit of darkness, sin, or self-pity, You came looking for us to bring us home to You, into Your loving arms of peace, safety, love, forgiveness, cleansing, and protection forever.

Father, thank You. Your love is real, and You care so deeply for us. Thank You, Lord, for chasing after us and not leaving us alone. I praise You for always thinking about us, and You will reveal Yourself to us in ways that draw us to You to know Your heart and love like never before. Lord, help us to turn over everything to You and trust Your love for us so that we never hide from You or keep things from You again.

Father, let Your love overcome any doubt, fear, or unbelief in our hearts. Let our love not be based on what our past was or how others may have or have not loved us. Let us base love on Your deep love for us always. Daddy God, we trust in You and Your love to keep us and continually reveal what true love looks like in Christ Jesus! In Jesus's name, Amen!

PRAYER

*M*any of my prayers and poems just came out of a heart that was so overwhelmed by the love of my Savior, Jesus Christ, forgiving someone like me who had lived such a sinful life. His love still overwhelms my heart with such joy and peace.

Lord,

I love You, Lord! Yes, I do! More than anyone or anything!
Thank You for comforting me,
     for loving me and taking care of me all the time.
Thank You for being true to Your children
     always, never failing us.
And, oh yes, Lord, we are forever failing You,
     but You never leave us to face things on our own.
     You are always there for me.
You give me strength at my weakest times.
     You are always picking me up
     and carrying me through the valleys,
     hand in hand, You and I.
I do love You, Lord.
You have given me new life,
     a purpose for living.
Even though now, at this time,
     I seem to have forgotten or
     put aside that purpose.

Oh, dear Lord, please lead me
    back to You and Your will for me.
    Give me courage and strength to
    stand firm in Your Word.
    Make me and yield me into
    the person You want me to be
    because I want to live Your will for my life,
    not my own.
Thank You, Lord!
In Jesus's name, Amen!

PRAYER OF DEEP THANKS

Lord,

I thank You for being my Savior, for giving Your precious life for me. I thank You for Your obedience to our heavenly Father's will.

I thank You for humbling Yourself to the humiliation of that day on the cross.

I thank You for being an example for us to live as You have lived.

I thank You for loving us enough to die on the cross.

I thank You for being so holy to have overcome sin and death only to rise again and live.

Yes, Lord, You live and are waiting for Your children to someday join You.

You took death to the grave,

And that's where it stayed.

Yet You, our Lord and Savior, arose.

I thank You for Your Helper, who You have so graciously left with us to guide us, to be our light from within, and to always comfort us.

Thank You, Lord, from within, for Your Helper, the Holy Spirit.

PRAYER FOR MY HUSBAND
THROUGH THE YEARS

One day the Lord spoke to me about praying daily for my husband. He gave me somewhat of the picture of Joseph when he was captured and enslaved, first by Potiphar and then imprisoned. God was with Joseph throughout the entire process. God's hand was on everything Joseph touched and did for his masters. His masters saw the hand of God on Joseph and knew it was his God who was blessing them through Joseph. Though Joseph was a slave and then in prison, God managed to promote him to the place of second in command in Egypt. God had a plan for Joseph to help His people. God has a plan for your husband to help your family too.

Prayer

Father, I pray for my husband. I pray that You give him favor in the eyes of those he works for and works with. I pray that You bless all that he touches and multiply all that he puts his hands and mind to do. I pray that You give him the skills, understanding, wisdom, ability, quickness, accuracy, and speed to do the things he is called to do each and every day. And to do it all with a heart of integrity and a spirit of excellency. I pray that You keep him awake, alert, and sober-minded on the job to prevent any type of injury or accident before it even happens.

I pray that You let his employers and coworkers see Your hand is upon him and know that it is You who is blessing them through him and want to keep him working for them for the entire period You would have him there. I pray for pay increases, that they see his worth and pay him accordingly. I pray You go before him and be his rear guard. Bless his going out and his coming in. I pray that he will be bold to speak of You and give You glory whenever asked about his abilities and/or job ethics.

I pray that no matter what is going on, that he keeps his eyes on You. Lord, I pray You keep him faithful to You and faithful in our marriage as he travels for each job. Put Your warring and protecting angels around him on every side, and put the fear of You in anyone who would come near him for harm, speak against him, or even look at him for harm; cause them to flee from him in a hundred ways. I bind all accidents, hurt, harm, danger, and injuries of any kind in the name of Jesus, and keep him safe every day. I pray the sun shall not smite him by day nor the moon by night. Lord, deliver him from all temptations and deceptions. Put Your favor around him like a shield.

Keep his eyes focused on Jesus, the author and finisher of his faith, and keep his mind stayed on You, Lord! Lord, raise him up to be the spiritual leader of this household, to hear Your voice above every other voice, binding all distractions, and filling him to overflow with Your Holy Spirit and be led by Your Spirit daily. Open his eyes of understanding to know the wisdom and knowledge of You, the hope of his calling in You, and the power of You working in and through him. Let him see Your hand at work daily in and through his life. Let him know Your love, goodness, and blessings on a deep and personal level every day, drawing him closer to You daily. In Jesus's mighty name, Amen!

PRAYER

Lord,

$\mathcal{H}$elp me, Holy Spirit, to speak Your words of truth
No matter if the person wants to hear truth or not.
But let Your words flow from a humble and loving heart
To show the person the same grace and mercy
You have shown me.
But even then, help me not be too hard or too soft.
Help me have the right balance of truth and grace.

Lord,

Help my ears to hear Your gentle guidance
To go to those whose hearts You desire to change.
And let Your rivers of living water
Flow freely from my mouth to their ears
To speak boldly Your truth that sets a person free.
Your truth that breathes new life into hearts.
Your truth that heals every broken spirit.
Your truth that sets every captive free.
Your truth that washes crimson as white as snow.

Use me, Lord, to touch lives for You.
Use me, Lord, to boldly declare
The gospel of Jesus with all I meet.
To let Your light shine brightly through the darkness.
To help those in bondage to addictions of any kind
to get free.

DONNA MCMILLIN

To speak Your words that will bring healing and
deliverance
And peace to every soul that is trapped in darkness.
Give me the tongue of the learned
To speak a word in season to those who are weary.
To be led by Your Spirit in all I do and say.
In Jesus's name I pray. Amen!

PRAYER

Lord,

$\mathcal{M}$y soul thirsts for You and You alone
And will not be satisfied with anything else.
I know because I tried to fill it with other things,
But no, nothing satisfies the longing of my soul like You!

My heart cries out to You
And longs for those precious times.
Times in Your presence filled with joy,
Times of hearing Your voice and
Sensing Your heartbeat and
Compassion for Your children.

Let my desires be Your desires.
Let my thoughts be Your thoughts.

Lord, only You can bring a true healing,
A healing of body, soul, mind, and heart!
You make us whole
spiritually, physically, mentally, and emotionally.
Only the blood of Jesus can do that!

Oh Lord, create in us a clean heart, and
Renew a loyal, steadfast spirit within us.
Lord, teach us and reveal to us
Your Word and truth by Your Holy Spirit.
Lead us in Your way of everlasting life
To know the depths of Your Word and love
And the revelation of who You truly are in Christ Jesus,
Our Savior and Lord!

DONNA MCMILLIN

Lord,

You are so mighty in all Your ways.
Your Word is life to those who trust in them.
You bring hope to the weary and brokenhearted.
Your Word is our Counselor at all times.
Your peace fills our hearts, souls, and minds.

Lord,

You are so wonderful to Your children.
Your mercy reaches beyond the farthest mountain.
Your love is never ending to those who fear You.
Your grace is greater than all our sins combined.
Your power gives us victory over every enemy.

Lord,

I cry out to You; fill us again and again.
Pour out Your Holy Spirit to breathe life into us.
Holy Spirit helps us to have a loyal heart to God.
Cleanse and purify our hearts continually before You
Make us aware of Your presence, always looking for You.
Teach us, Holy Spirit, give us more understanding
So that our hearts long for You, our God, only!
Draw us closer to You to know You deeper.
We want to know the richness and depths of Your heart.
Fill us, Holy Spirit, so we may do the work of our Father,
To follow in the footsteps of our Savior, Jesus Christ,
Who chose obedience to the cross
to bring us life everlasting.
In Jesus's name, Amen!

PRAYER

Lord,

Our hearts are Yours; make us to know Your way.
Our lives are Yours; make us to walk in Your way.
We surrender our all to our loving and faithful God.
Lord, we trust in Your goodness toward us.
We trust in Your marvelous and wonderful works to us,
And we say Your kingdom come, Your will be done
In every area of our lives here on earth as it is in heaven.

We trust Your unfailing love and know Your way is
What is best for us and will glorify You!
We love You, Lord God and Savior, we love You!

Lord,

You are almighty and all powerful,
Yet You pour out Your compassion
And goodness over us with all gentleness.
You are holy and righteous,
Yet You apply the blood of Jesus
To cleanse us and give us Your righteousness.
You are awesome and wonderful!
How great You are toward us!
So amazing! Beyond what words can describe!
Lord, let our lives be a holy sacrifice before You,
And let us be obedient to Your every word!
Lord, help us to have a loyal heart to You
All the days of our lives, until we come home to You!
In Jesus's name, Amen.

DONNA MCMILLIN

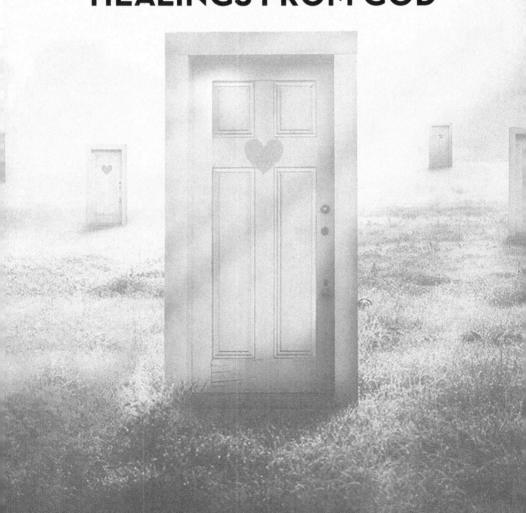

Section 3

TESTIMONIES AND HEALINGS FROM GOD

MY TESTIMONY

*P*art of my testimony I shared in the preface, but here I go back to before the day I walked into that church and God turned my life around.

I do not have a lot of memories growing up, but I do remember going to church with my parents and siblings over the years. I remember going to church camp one summer and having a great time. I got baptized several times at a church we attended during some of the older elementary years of my life. It seems to me I thought every time I sinned, I needed to get baptized. That was my understanding of what I heard, not necessarily what was preached. Growing up I felt like God was up in heaven shaking His head and pointing His finger at me every time I messed up. I thought more along the condemning line, not understanding His great love at that time. So I did not have any type of personal relationship with Jesus Christ because I did not even know He wanted a personal relationship with me. I really did not know of His love for me and definitely did not think He loved me.

When I was ten years old, my dad and mom got divorced after twenty-seven years of marriage and thirteen children together. Marriage is a wonderful covenant God designed between a man and a woman, but sometimes marriages can fail for all kinds of reasons. Those of us kids who remained at home lived with my mom, who worked the night shift at her job. We were by ourselves in the evenings quite a bit with some of our older siblings. About half our siblings had already married and moved out of the house by this time.

We moved to Kentucky when I was fifteen years old. I met someone I thought to become instant friends with. One night changed my life forever. Against my better judgment, I went for a ride with this friend and a couple of men I did not know. I was taken advantage of sexually and blamed myself because I had drunk beer for the first time in my life and passed out. I knew that God designed sexual intimacy to be pure and only within the covenant of marriage between a man and a woman.

Soon afterward, I attempted suicide by taking a huge bottle of aspirin. Thankfully, it did not work. At this time in my life, I had no idea about the love of Jesus and His forgiveness through faith in His death on the cross. I began to live a life full of shame and guilt, turning to alcohol and drugs. I could not even look at myself in the mirror unless I was drunk. On the outside, I tried to look like I was happy, but on the inside, I was miserable. I hated myself and my life. Drugs and alcohol were not the answer and did nothing to help me find the peace in my heart and soul that only a relationship with Jesus can do. I remember thinking that I had to go live with my dad because I just had this feeling inside of me that if I did not, I would not live through my teenage years into adulthood.

So I moved to Indiana with my dad and stepmom and her girls when I was in the tenth grade. For a time, things were better. But I fell into that same trap of the enemy and started drinking again to cover up the pain. I finally graduated high school and decided to follow my two oldest brothers into the US Marine Corps.

I graduated from boot camp as the honor grad of my platoon. I then went to school for my military occupation skill (MOS) in North Carolina. While in the marines, I again started drinking and living a worldly life. I was in the top five of our class at school, so I got to pick my duty station, which was Marine Corps Air Station, Kaneohe Bay, Hawaii. When I got there, I was told not to stay in the sun for long because of the powerful sunrays in Hawaii. However, I did not listen, went to the beach, drank heavily, and ended up falling asleep and getting an extreme sunburn. I could not go to work the next day and was written up by my master sergeant for damaging government property (as mentioned earlier in the book, my body was considered government property). But my master sergeant was very fair, and after a year or so, he took it off my record.

I received a couple of meritorious promotions, but I continued to drink and do drugs to forget how miserable I was because of the rape when I was fifteen. It took me a very long time to admit that it was rape because I felt it was my fault because I was drinking.

I started seeing another marine, and he ended up asking me to marry him. I said yes, and we were married shortly afterward. A few years later, I discovered I was pregnant when I started having great pains in my abdomen and began spotting. I went to the military ER, and they rushed me into surgery with an ectopic pregnancy (the baby was stuck in the fallopian tube). I lost the baby, and it was devastating for both of us.

In 1986, my oldest nephew was killed stateside in a car accident at the age of thirteen. I was devastated. One of my sisters worked it out with the Red Cross to contact my base and fix it so I could go back to his funeral. At the funeral, I heard he had been saved several months before the accident. I did not understand what it meant to be saved and wondered about it. I remember, though, that it was that day at the funeral I thought I truly wanted to stop drinking and doing drugs. For two years, I tried and tried to stop, but I could not on my own.

I finally got out of the marines, and we went back to Pennsylvania, where my husband was from, to live with his family because we were trying to work things out in our marriage. I ended up with another ectopic pregnancy, only this time my tube ruptured internally, and I had surgery again. I stayed in the hospital for a week. No one was able to come to see me because my family all lived in other states. When I got out of the hospital, my husband said he wanted a divorce.

I drove from Pennsylvania to Kentucky to live with my mom. For the fourth time, I attempted suicide and ended up in the hospital. The chaplain came around and asked if I wanted to talk about it. But because of all the shame and guilt, I could not bring myself to open up about myself. Unfortunately, our marriage did not work out, and we got a divorce.

I reenlisted in the marines and was stationed in Nashville, Tennessee. I had to go to a weeklong training in Evansville, Indiana, and met my future husband, Jim, there. I was not yet a Christian, and neither was he, so the beginning of our relationship did not start according to what a godly relationship should look like. The day before leaving, he pulled me into his office and asked me if we had started a relationship. I thought, *Oh my goodness, this is the most goober man I have ever met.*

A month or so later, I told a friend that something told me I was going to spend the rest of my life with this man, but I did not want it. You see, I had just gotten divorced and was hurt by life. We did start seeing each other. He ended up taking me to meet his parents in Colorado and asked me to marry him six months later. At first, I said yes; but when I got home, I called him and broke it off. I was dating another marine at the time who lived out of state. I had no morals really and was loaded down with so much shame and guilt from my past.

Then in January 1988, I finally went to church with my coworkers and their families. I heard the gospel message of Jesus Christ as the Son of God. That day I learned how He died on the cross for my sins and rose again on the third day so that we could have forgiveness and eternal life. I gave my life to the Lord and was baptized in February 1988.

Then in March of 1988, I got a call from that goober man who had asked me to marry him. His grandmother was having surgery to amputate her legs, and he called to see if he could talk to me. We could always talk to each other pretty easily. So we talked and ended up getting back together. We got married in April 1989. God had healed me from many things, and I was set free from drugs and alcohol. I never went back to them again, praise the Lord! But as a baby Christian, I had a lot of growing and healing to do. My husband was a baby Christian as well, so we were both new to our faith in Jesus Christ. We stumbled for months learning how to get along. It was a rough road.

In September 1989, I was going in for same-day nasal surgery for a deviated septum and to clear out my nasal passages. Three weeks before the surgery, I was praying and felt in my spirit something was going to happen with the surgery. But I heard the Lord whisper to me, "Trust Me." So I did. When I went in that day for surgery, they gave me a little something to calm me before surgery. I do not remember going back to the surgery room. When they administered the anesthesia, I died on the operating table, and code blue went off in the hospital. The timing of God is perfect because as soon as code blue went off, a cardiologist had just walked out of the surgery room next to mine and came directly into my operating room. The medical team had to do CPR and use the defibrillator paddles on me three times to revive me.

When they finally revived me, only 17 percent of my heart was working; the whole left side had shut down. They had me on five medicines to just keep me alive, a heart catheter, oxygen, a tube down my nose into my lungs and stomach to drain the fluid that built up when I died, and IVs. The staff tied my arms down so when I came to, I did not panic and try to pull loose. They almost lost me again that same night. They came out and told my husband what happened about two hours later. They informed him

DONNA MCMILLIN

that I needed either a heart transplant or open-heart surgery to survive, but they did not know if I would even survive the night.

My husband called my family, and they came to the hospital. My mom came into my room and told me she was going to start living for the Lord again like I had been telling her. However, she said she was going to need me to help her live for the Lord, and I needed to live to do so. I remember thinking at that point, because I could not really talk, *Okay, Lord, this is why this happened, and I am ready to live again.*

The hospital did not have the facilities needed to do the heart transplant or open-heart surgery that I might need. After talking to my husband and family, they flew me in a helicopter the next morning to a hospital renowned for its heart facility in Nashville. When they brought me into the ER at the new hospital, they wheeled an older woman out who was also there for heart problems.

The doctors did not know what was causing my heart failure. They tested my blood several times a day and did heart ultrasounds every day. The anesthesiologist told me they had me on a heart medicine that would bring a dead man back to life, but it was not doing anything for me. They did a heart biopsy. They continued to run test after test but getting no answers as to why this happened. And nothing was helping me improve. My family prayed constantly. I was covered in prayer from the East Coast to the West Coast and the South to the North. My dad had heart disease and felt like this was his fault, but it was not.

I eventually had a transfusion of two pints of blood. It seemed from that point on, I started improving little by little. My husband commented the blood transfusion was working like Jesus's blood on the cross cleanses and heals us.

One day the Christian doctor came in and told me there was a twenty-eight-year-old woman, a wife and mother, who came into their hospital ER with same thing, and she died. I wrote her family a poem/letter and asked the doctor to give it to them.

Day after day, they administered tests but got no answers. But after the blood transfusion, they removed the tube from my nose on the fifth day. Until then, I had nothing to eat or drink, just ice chips on my lips. On the eighth day, one of the doctors came in with a very baffled look on his face and said that the ultrasound looked as if nothing had ever happened to my heart. My husband jumped up and shouted, "It's a miracle from God!"

The doctor mumbled, "Well, somebody up there likes you," and left the room. The anesthesiologist and the Christian doctor both said it was a miracle because nothing they did was helping me; they were only trying to keep me alive. On the tenth day, I walked out of that hospital with absolutely nothing wrong with my heart. That was thirty-five years ago. You see, it was a miracle.

Two months later, I had to go back for a follow-up. The young woman doing my heart ultrasound said she did not understand why I needed the test because my heart was just as good as hers. In that moment, I shared the miracle of how God healed my heart. My husband and I would tell anyone who would listen how God truly performed a great miracle that day and completely healed me. As mentioned earlier, heart disease runs in my family. My oldest brother died in 1996, at the age of forty-eight, of a massive heart attack. My dad died in 1998, at the age of seventy-two, of a massive heart attack. One of my brothers had to have a nine-bypass heart surgery. Another had ten stents put in and because they could not do more, he had to have a two-bypass heart surgery. He now has an internal heart defibrillator.

I have never had another issue with my heart. I taught group exercise classes for eighteen years, just ending this year. I have run three marathons and six half-marathons, coming in first place in my female age group in one of the half-marathons. And in my second marathon, I qualified, just barely, for the Boston Marathon. I have done six tough mudders, one duathlon, and several other small running races. All praise goes to the Lord for allowing me to do this and for being alive today. My heart is still doing great, and I know it is because the Lord healed me completely.

In February 2012, I fell down my many basement steps, actually flew down my stairs. My sister, Bonny, and her husband, Chip, had just left after visiting from Tennessee regarding my upcoming mission trip to Haiti in July 2012. We had such a good time of fellowship. The Lord really was present during their visit. She and I were texting back and forth. I wanted her to know how much growth I was seeing in her because of her relationship with Jesus. I finally had to stop texting because it was Saturday, and I needed to finish laundry and get prepared for church the next day. So I started down my stairs, and the heel of my boot got caught on a nail that was sticking up. I just started flying in the air. I remembered Jim was working out of town, and I was home alone. I thought, *Lord, please don't let me die down here alone.*

I hit my head on the concrete floor. I heard a loud smack and thought, *Oh no, this might be bad.* That was the last thing I remember for a few minutes. The doctors think I was out maybe five minutes or so, but I woke up. I had put my phone in my sweater pocket before going downstairs, and it had flown out of my pocket and skittered across the basement floor. When I woke up, I wondered, *Why is everything black and white?* I started to stand but had to stop because the whole room was spinning. I knew I had to call for help, so I crawled over to my phone. I know it was by the grace of God that I was able to call my friend Cathy, though I do not remember dialing her number. When she answered, I told her that I had just flown down my basement stairs and needed help. She was so concerned and worried.

I hung up and could feel wetness coming out of my ear. I knew immediately it was blood. I also felt my head was leaning over to my left side and thought, *I better not move it too much because something might be broken in my neck or spine.* When you are in shock, you do not think straight. I did not think to immediately call 911. All I could think was, *If Cathy called someone to come over and help, my front door is locked, and no one will be able to get in. And I don't want them breaking it down.* So I crawled military style up my basement stairs to the kitchen floor because again, I could not walk; everything was still spinning.

As soon as I got into the kitchen, my friend Sean returned my call from before I fell. When I answered, I told him several times, "Sean, I can't talk I just fell down my basement stairs." He immediately asked me if I called 911, but I just repeated what I said. So he said he was calling 911 and hung up. I crawled to my front door to unlock it. Then I thought, *Blood is coming out of my ear, and I don't want blood on my carpet.* Then I crawled back to the kitchen floor.

My dog, Gracey, was here at the time. When I crawled up the stairs, she was standing at the top, just staring at me. I think I let her out or something; I don't remember. But finally, friends from church showed up, and the ambulance came. I did not realize it until the ambulance arrived that my wrist was broken and zigzagged in an odd shape. But no bones were coming out of my skin, thank the Lord. I ended up with a broken right wrist, broken left collarbone—a nonunion break—a broken left inner-ear bone, a skull fracture from my left ear up the side of my head and across my forehead, and a concussion. I kept throwing up because of the dizziness that stayed with me until May 2012.

Anyway, after the first surgery on my wrist, someone had to take care of me because I had both arms in a sling and was dizzy as you can get not being able to stand alone or anything. My sister Pam took me home with her to Tennessee to stay for a week, until Jim could get away from work. She had to bathe me, feed me, and do everything for me. It was somewhat humiliating. Then my friend Shelia came to take me home, pick up my mother-in-law from the airport, and drive us home because my mother-in-law was going to stay with me until Jim got home. Then my mother-in-law had to bathe me. Oh my, even further humiliation!

July was supposed to be my mission trip to Haiti. I had sent letters to family and friends about helping to pay for the trip. At the time, I worked at a local gym and local university teaching group exercise classes and personal training. When I was at my sister's house, I was thinking, *Well Lord, I believe You were leading me to go on the mission trip, but what am I going to do now?* It did not look like I was going to be able to go because this was going to be a long healing process. I would at some time need surgery on my left shoulder for the break, but first, it was going to take time for my wrist to heal because of the severity of the fracture.

The second day I was at my sister's house, I was down about maybe not being able to go on the mission trip to Haiti. And lo and behold, our church secretary texted me saying she had received such a sweet letter and check for my Haiti mission trip from a friend who took my group exercises classes. I texted back that it was sweet. And she texted back saying, "No, Donna, you don't understand. They paid for your entire mission trip fare." I was so overwhelmed and excited. All I could do was shout to the Lord and thank Him. I realized He was going to allow me to go on the mission trip. I was able to go on that mission trip with the help of all my friends who were also on the mission trip, carrying my luggage everywhere the entire trip. And I was so blessed by it.

Let me step back a minute and tell you about a miracle involving my broken inner ear. While in the ER, the ENT doctor did not say anything to me about what he feared would happen to my hearing. But he thought I could lose some hearing in that ear. Well, a friend from church's father was visiting from out of state. In the past, we had talked quite a bit. My friend had told him of my fall and the damage it caused to my body. He walked over to me in church and said that the Holy Spirit told him to come over and lay hands on my ears and pray for healing with no hearing loss. I was very open and said, "Yes, please do." As he laid hands on me and prayed, I truly felt the power of the Lord and knew this was of God.

Two weeks later, I had to do a hearing test and then return to the ENT doctor for results and follow-up. The ENT doctor read the test and said that I barely had any noticeable hearing loss at all. He told me that when he saw me in the ER, he thought I would have at least a 50 percent hearing loss and maybe even up to 80 percent hearing loss. However, I had barely any noticeable hearing loss. I told him what happened at church, and he said he believed it. Another miracle from God.

I had four total surgeries from February 2012 to March 2013, I believe. I had a setback with my two-part surgery, but it was not bad. The Lord has blessed me to have fully recovered from it. During my occupational therapy, the occupational therapist told me that I probably would never be able to do a regular push-up again, and I thought, *Oh yeah, well watch and see because my God can do anything.* I am able to do regular push-ups, not the girl style but the guy style. God is so good!

God has healed my marriage. God knew who to bring into my life, even though at the time I was not ready for him. But God knew who I needed. The first fifteen years of our marriage were very rough for me. My husband would always begin his prayers—and still does—thanking the Lord for His love for us and our love for each other. In the beginning of our marriage, I wondered, *What love for each other are you talking about?* But God did a mighty work in my heart and in his heart too. We are more in love now than ever before. We have been married for thirty-five years, and I thank the Lord daily for the man He has given me to share my life with.

My husband had testicular cancer in 1998, six months after my dad died. He had to have radiation for about six to eight weeks, but God has healed him with no more cancer! We were unable to have children, and that devastated me for quite some time. Finally, some years ago, I was able to release that pain and disappointment to the Lord and trust in His unfailing love. As I wrote earlier in this book, God gave me a dream several years ago in which my pastor told me to read 1 Samuel 1:1–8. This is the passage about Hannah being unable to get pregnant and her husband asking if he wasn't better than ten sons. When I awoke, I knew the Lord was speaking to me, saying that He would be better to me than ten sons and would cause my husband to be better to me than ten sons. And God has been faithful in that.

My husband, Jim, was in the first Desert Storm War in 1990. He and his unit were on the front lines, on the ground. We were all constantly praying for him and my oldest living brother, who was over there too. It was surely a trying time, but our hope and trust were in the Lord. I praise the Lord for bringing them both home safe and sound.

Our marriage has not been perfect, and we have continued to have ups and downs like every marriage. But I am telling you in these last five to six years, God has done a great healing in our marriage, drawing us closer to Him and to each other. God is faithful. Life is not easy, but God is always there with us, walking us through every circumstance in life. He never leaves us alone or forsakes us. He lifts us up and carries us through the toughest times.

I remember going through early menopause (at the time I did not realize that's what it was) and feeling like my emotions were unbalanced, I told my husband about it. I constantly prayed and asked the Lord if I needed to see a counselor. I also prayed for healing. But I heard Him softly whisper to me, "I am your wonderful Counselor. Let Me be your Counselor." I did, and He brought me through it with more strength and faith in Him as my healer and deliverer.

In the entry titled "Jesus Never Fails," found after this portion of my testimony, I speak of a time in 2015 when Jim was having severe chest pains. The Lord walked us through that time. Well, a similar situation happened again on Tuesday, July 18, 2023. Jim was at work and started having even more severe chest pains and sweating profusely in an air-conditioned office. He had forgotten his nitroglycerin pills. I believe someone called for the EMTs on site. They gave him nitroglycerin and were pretty sure (and Jim was too) that Jim was having a heart attack. The pain started going into Jim's jaw and neck, and he knew what was happening. He began to pray,

"God Your will be done. Heal me, but I trust You for Your will to be done."
And he prayed that I would be okay.

The EMTs had called the ambulance. They picked him up and took
him to the hospital closest to the worksite. During the ride to the hospital,
the ambulance personnel showed Jim on the EKG where he was having
a heart attack. As soon as they got him to the hospital, the hospital staff
had already prepared his room to take his vitals and do the angioplasty
procedure immediately. They saw the blockage. This time it was 100
percent blockage in the right coronary artery, where the stent was placed in
2015. So they cleaned it out, removed the old stent, and put in two bigger
additional stents to have a wider opening for him.

During this time, I was at home because Jim was working out of town.
The administrator for his work called me and asked if anyone had called
to let me know what was going on. No one had. She explained everything.
This time, nervousness did creep in, not from a position of panic, but
because of the two-hour distance between us. I started praying right away.
I had to make many phone calls, first to the coworker who was with Jim to
see what was going on and then to our pastor, my family, and Jim's family
for them to all start praying immediately. God is so good because we
know He orchestrated the timeliness of the reaction of everyone involved
in helping him get the medical attention he needed. We praise God that it
was just a mild heart attack, and because of His timing and putting people
in the right place at the right time, Jim is doing much better. We praise
the Lord for His faithfulness and healing.

Here's another testimony of God's faithfulness. Romans 8:28 states,
"And we know that all things work together for good to those who love
God, to those who are the called according to His purpose." I love this
verse because it reminds me of Jesus giving me this verse as a promise when
we were in the marines, moving from North Carolina to Nashville. We still
had our house in Indiana along with its mortgage and electricity bills, and
moving to Nashville meant we would have to pay rent and utilities to live
at a place there. I was worried because with Jim's military pay, we could not
afford it ourselves. As I prayed about it one day, the Holy Spirit spoke this
verse as a promise to me that He would work all things out for good for
me and Jim because we loved Him. And more important, He loved us and
called us to salvation in Jesus Christ and His purpose. He promised me He

would provide three things: a place to stay, a church to worship and join, and a job to provide the extra income for us. And God did just that. I was the first one to get to Nashville because Jim was overseas but would be there soon. I stayed with one of my sisters and brother-in-law for a month or so, looking for a place to live, a church, and a job. God began, one by one, bringing His promises to pass by providing a condo to rent. It was owned by a Christian, and the rent was close to $200 cheaper than those in the same complex around us. We moved in and then visited many churches. But the Lord led us to the one we joined where we felt His presence and like part of a family. Lastly, He provided me a dream job of working for the Baptist Sunday School Board in the sales department. With my salary and bonuses, He helped us to where we could afford our house payment and utilities in Indiana and our rent and utilities in Nashville. God gives us promises when we seek Him and give Him our plans and desires and worries. And then He fulfills every promise He gives us from His Word! Believe me, I did not know how we were going to do it. I went to the Lord as my only source for answers and provision. Praise the Lord, God heard my prayers and gave me a promise, which He fulfilled. Trust Him that this verse, and every word in the Bible, is true, and He is faithful!

There are so many things I could write about His faithfulness and goodness to me and my husband and our families, but it would take forever to tell and so much room to write. I just want to encourage you to go to the Lord Jesus Christ in prayer, cry out to Him with your cares and concerns, and He will answer you. He will heal and provide every need. No, it may not be easy, but His grace is sufficient, and His strength is enough as He is our Rock and our anchor. Trust Jesus for all your needs and struggles. With Him all things are possible. His love is everlasting and enough to send His only begotten Son, Jesus Christ, to die on the cross for the sins (yours and mine) of the world, defeating death and sin once and for all. He rose from the dead three days later and is now seated at the right hand of God.

Jesus said in John 14:6, "I am the Way, the Truth, and the Life. No man comes to the Father but through Me." It is by His grace that we are saved, not by anything we could do, but a gift He gives to us of eternal life. If we confess with our mouths Jesus as Lord and believe in our hearts that God raised Him from the dead, we will be saved: "For with the heart one believes unto righteousness, and with the mouth confession is made unto salvation" (Romans 10:10). Repent and be baptized in the name of the Father, Son, and Holy Spirit, and walk into a new life through faith in Jesus Christ as Savior. Surrender your life to Him as Lord of your life, dying to self and sin and living to Jesus daily. Let the Holy Spirit of God be your guide, teacher, deliverer, counselor, Helper, Comforter, strength, peace, hope, joy, lover of your soul, and the One you depend on every day to live a life pleasing to our God and Father! Let the power of the Holy Spirit, with the baptism of the Holy Spirit, fill you each and every day to walk by faith on this earth in your daily life and be found faithful to Him! The same resurrection power of the Holy Spirit lives in you and me to give us the power to overcome sin and temptations and come out victorious over the enemy daily! Trust in God's unfailing love, and surrender your all to Him! You can trust Him with your heart, life, family, and future.

GOD'S NEVER-FAILING PRESENCE AND POWER

I was meditating on God's goodness in my life and how He has moved so powerfully when I remembered a season while I was stationed in North Carolina. Today, God revealed how He walked me through it.

My husband had to go overseas to a duty station for eighteen months, and I could not go with him. We had to drive four hours from our military base housing to the airport he would fly out of to his duty station. On the way home, I was angry with God for us having to be separated so long and him so far away again. I was talking to the Lord, complaining and even telling the Lord how mad I was at Him, and He showed me a picture of me lying on the floor throwing a temper tantrum just like a child not getting their way. It sobered me up and I thought, *Oh my goodness, Lord, is that really me?* He responded, "Yes Donna, that's really you." So the rest of the way home, I repented and prayed for God's strength to get us both through this time away from each other. And you know what? Looking back at it now, God used that picture to give me the strength to trust Him and know He was with us both and would see us through this time of separation. And the Lord did. Jesus never fails!

> Trust in and rely confidently on the Lord with all your heart and do not rely on your own insight or understanding. In all your ways know and acknowledge and recognize Him, and He will make your paths straight and smooth [removing obstacles that block your way]. (Proverbs 3:5–6 AMP)

> Blessed [gratefully praised and adored] be the God and Father of our Lord Jesus Christ, the Father of mercies and the God of all comfort. (2 Corinthians 1:3 AMP)

Let your character [your moral essence, your inner nature] be free from the love of money [shun greed-be financially ethical] being content with what you have; for <u>He has said, "I will never [under any circumstances] desert you [nor give you up nor leave you without support, nor will I in any degree leave you helpless], Nor will I forsake or let you down or relax My hold on you [assuredly not]!"</u> (Hebrews 13:5 AMP)

JESUS NEVER FAILS

*A*bout nine years ago, we came home from church on a Wednesday night. We were getting ready for bed when my husband started having some chest pains and other signs of a heart attack. Because he works in safety, he recognized all the signs, and he knew what to do in these circumstances. So, I asked him if I needed to call 911. He did not answer. I knew and recognized the signs as well. Somehow, God kept me very calm in this situation. (God's grace is sufficient comes to mind.) So I called 911. The ambulance came and took him to the emergency room. I followed in my vehicle.

I called our friends, Pastor Mike and Cathy, to let them know what was going on. We got to the ER, and they took my husband back to a room. While I was in the waiting room, Pastor Mike and Cathy arrived. Pastor Mike began to pray, and I tell you it was like the Holy Spirit whispered Isaiah 26:3–4, which appears at the end of this first section. In my heart I knew no matter what happened, everything was going to be OK, and I had the greatest peace. I did not have this verse memorized at the time, but yearly I read the Bible from front to back. So, the scripture where Jesus said the Holy Spirit will teach you all things of Me, and He will comfort you (John 14:26) came to pass right there in the ER waiting room. The Holy Spirit brought that scripture up in my spirit out of the place it was stored from reading the Word of God all these years.

The medical team let us go back to the room with my husband. His chest pains had subsided a lot. They had him hooked up to an EKG monitor. At one point, they were going to let him go home, but he started having chest pains again. So they decided to keep him overnight. His chest pain continued throughout the night, so they gave him nitroglycerin several times. The next morning, they did a heart catheter in his arm and found he had a 98 percent blockage in his right coronary artery, which is extremely dangerous. They put in a stent at that time.

God is so good to us. Jesus did not fail us in this situation at all. Just the fact that my husband began to have chest pains before we went to bed instead of when he was asleep was amazing to us. The timing was a gift from the Lord that prevented him from dying in his sleep. The sudden onset of chest pains just as they were going to release him, causing the hospital to keep him overnight for observation and the procedure in the morning, was also a great blessing from the Lord. God took care of my husband and me completely. We kept our minds fixed on Jesus, trusted He was in control, and He kept us in His perfect peace. Jesus never fails!

> You will keep him in perfect peace, whose mind is stayed on You, because he trusts in You. Trust in the Lord forever, for in Yah, the Lord, is everlasting strength. (Isaiah 26:3–4 NKJV)

Included in this section are the testimonies of my blood sisters and church sisters.

I am so blessed to have the sisters that I have in my family, and they are sisters in Christ also. I feel like God really knit us together in our hearts and in our faith in Jesus Christ as our Savior and Lord. I thank the Lord daily for them and their close friendships. I praise God that they love Jesus and are known by Him!

I am also blessed to have sisters in the Lord at church. I thank the Lord daily for them also.

This first one is from my sister, Judy. Judy played a very big role in praying me into the kingdom of God! When I first got saved, she and her husband, Ricky, told me living a Christian life was not always easy, and I would still go through things in life. That was the best thing anyone could have told me.

As a little girl, Mom always took us to church, so we learned who Jesus was at a young age. So growing up we knew we had to be saved and baptized to go to heaven. I remember going to church and having to learn the books of the Bible and the girls (sisters Wanda, me, Bonny, Betty) would sing in front of church. The church people always clapped for us. So I knew who Jesus was, but as you get older, I guess you just take things for granted. As I got older, our pastor had been preaching from Ephesians, and I began listening better and trying to understand better. He would say, "Do you really know Jesus? Stay in your Word, read your Bible every day, give everything to God." So when I was around sixty years of age, even though I knew who God was, I was really beginning to understand who He was! I rededicated my life to God!

My special time with God is when I go to bed. Everybody has gone to bed, and it is nice and quiet, so I just say, "God, this is Your and my time." Even though I know He hears everyone, I also know He is with me. So now, each night I give it all to God to take care of. He said we should do that, and He would take care of things. So, when I lay my head down now, I fall asleep without running all those worries through my head. My only regret is that I waited till I was sixty to get it! I lost a lot of time with Him and all the blessings He gives out!

This second testimony is from my sister, Bonny. In my teenage years, I babysat her two young boys.

In the Middle is what the book would be titled if I were to write one. I was the middle child out of thirteen.

I got married at a young age and divorced at a young age. The marriage lasted seven years and brought me two beautiful children. I thought marriage was supposed to last a lifetime. But the marriage failed and not only changed my life but my thinking too, which I allowed to turn to bitterness.

In reflecting on that time, I have come to understand that I did not follow God's plan for my life; I did what I wanted to do. I was not honoring the Fifth Commandment: "Honor your mother and father." Our home was dysfunctional. Our parents were fighting all the time. They were strict and did not trust us. And one did not know the Lord until later in life. So getting married at a young age was my rebellion, and the consequences were mine too. It was not until I was in my second marriage and third child that I had a come-to-Jesus moment through a Bible study called "Experiencing God." And I experienced God in the early 1990s. My blind eyes were given spiritual eyes, and I saw that God was a loving God who had pursued me to be His very own child. I can remember that day turned from darkness to light. I was blind, but now I see. I began putting God's truths in my mind and heart and what He says about me as a child of God.

I do not want to give Satan any credit, but God's Word says Satan came to destroy, and Jesus came to give us eternal life. As I have grown closer to God in my walk, Satan has tried every tactic to make me fall away by going after my children and grandchildren. So, as I am trusting and believing God will do what He says He will do in His time, I am not going to sway from His promises! I know He has been with me all my life, and He will never leave me. I have had my ups and downs, my heart broken more than once, and my health to be examined, and I am still following after what I know has gotten me to this point in my life, a personal relationship with Jesus Christ. Today I have a godly husband who wants to honor God too. So together we are not navigating this life/marriage without Him.

For this is how God loved the world: He gave His one and only Son, so that everyone who believes in Him will not perish but have eternal life. God sent His Son into the world not to judge the world, but to save the world through Him. (John 3:16–17 NLT)

Jesus said, "yes, I am the vine; you are the branches. Those who remain in Me, and I in them, will produce much fruit. For apart from Me you can do nothing." (John 15:5 NLT)

"For I know the plans I have for you," says the Lord. "They are plans for good and not disaster, to give you a future and a hope. In those days when you pray, I will listen. If you look for Me wholeheartedly, you will find Me." (Jeremiah 29:11–13 NLT)

But you are not like that, for you are a chosen people. You are royal priests, a holy nation, God's very own possession. As a result, you can show others the goodness of God, for He called you out of the darkness into His wonderful light. (1 Peter 2:9 NLT)

"Goodness of God" by Bethel Music*
I love You, Lord.
Oh, Your mercy never fails me.
All my days
I've been held in Your hands
From the moment that I wake up
Until I lay my head.
Oh, I will sing of the goodness of God

*This song and these words are a testimony of my life. I will always sing of the goodness of God!

Bonny Boyd Carrier
The Middle Child

This one is from my twin sister, Dottie. I am ten minutes older than Dottie. Moma had a cousin who had twins who looked just alike, so when she got pregnant with us, she prayed and prayed we would not look alike, and we do not look alike. God sure answered Moma's prayers.

Dottie's Testimony

Now that I can laugh and joke, I say that I pushed Donna on out and said, "You try it first, and I'll see you in ten minutes." I had similar experiences as my twin and did try alcohol. But I never liked it enough to become addicted (by God's grace) as I did not like the feeling of being out of control.

I grew up very fast as though I was a grownup at age thirteen and took on many responsibilities. I always had low self-esteem and never felt good enough. I experienced many of the things my twin sister did, and it caused me to basically just exist. I went from one relationship to another looking for love, not sure of love from my family or whomever. I was married several times and had my son at the age of twenty-five. I knew he was a gift from God as I always wanted to be a mom.

I always worked hard and took care of myself as best I could as I had moved out from home when I was eighteen. My marriages failed because I never put God first in my life. I know that without my family's prayers, I would not be here today. I did end up giving my life back to the Lord.

I experienced some things that were brought on by someone who was supposed to be trustworthy but ended up betraying my trust. It took me years to forgive myself. I ended up going to Al-Anon and finding the love of God through the people there and the meetings I attended. When our mom was dying of COPD in 2010, I realized I wanted to be with Moma in heaven and knew I wanted to make my relationship with Jesus stronger. I started attending church again and belong to it today. I know I am forgiven and saved through faith in Jesus Christ as the Son of God, who loved me enough to die for me on the cross and rose again on the third day. I have found a true love with the Lord that has helped heal me from all the bad relationships in my life. I am growing very much in my walk with the Lord, learning God's love is forever and true. He has washed me white as snow! Thank You, Jesus!

This one is from my sister Pam. We lived very close to Pam and her husband and boys while stationed in Nashville. We were able to see each other often during those three years.

When we were growing up, no one ever asked you, "What's your name?" What did they always ask you? What number were you, and I was number 10. I have always said, "One day I'm going to write a book titled, *I Am a 10.*

Being number 10 meant that I did not get a lot of Moma time, so my oldest sister kind of became my mom. I was extremely independent and on my own a lot at a young age. I remember spending the night in my car at times because I did not have the gas money to drive home and get back to school the next day. I always said when I was younger that I had a will of iron. I remember Daddy and Moma teaching us that dynamite comes in small packages and telling us we could do anything. So I have always held that mentality—that I have been able to do anything I wanted to do.

I always gave credit to myself until later in life. I realized that the footsteps behind me were those of God following me and carrying me when I could not carry myself. I am grateful that our parents took us to church because we had the foundation of knowing right from wrong. I have always had that moral compass and that line in the sand, knowing never to cross that line. And as I have gotten older, it has been my responsibility to enrich my relationship with Jesus. I am still growing every day, but no, I would not be here if not for the love of Jesus Christ and the forgiveness of my sins that He offers and His help to walk forward every day.

This testimony is from my friend and sis in the Lord, Shavon. Shavon is always smiling, and her faith in the Lord is strong.

In 2002, at the age of twenty-three, I became a single mother and was in a toxic relationship. At that time, I considered myself a churchgoer, but I still didn't have a genuine relationship with God. I would continue to go to church despite going through my trials and many tribulations. One day at church God spoke into my life through a pastor, and that turned my life around. The pastor began to declare the plans and purposes that God had for my life. I decided to rededicate my life to the Lord. I started praying and reading the Word of God for myself. The things that pulled me away from God, I began to let those things and people go. God healed my heart and showed me that I can love again. He blessed me with my amazing husband of eighteen years and three wonderful children. I'm so glad I didn't give up on God, and He didn't give up on me. I stood on this scripture, Psalm 37:5: "Commit thy way unto the Lord and he shall give thee the desires of your heart."

With God, so many of my heart's desires have come to pass, and for that, I am forever grateful. I thank God for loving me and keeping me. God's way will always be the best way. God bless you, my sister Donna, for taking the time to share a snippet of my testimony. I am so proud of you, Donna. Congratulations on your book.

My Family Tribute: The Lives We All Lived

From birth, our lives were intertwined.
Even more, lives together by God's design.
Each character and personality so unique.
Each child, to our parents, a great intrigue.

The lives we all lived
Were all we had to give.
We lived lives that were full,
Lives with so much pull.

Lives that always connected.
Lives that always corrected.
Lives that stood together.
Lives that withstood the weather.

Storms surrounded us at times.
Winds blowing like chimes.
At times causing great pain,
But how God granted its gain.

Each life took form in binding love.
A wife, a husband that fit like a glove.
The Lord blessed with children to abound.
There was no lack of love to be found.

Families expanded, growing the family tree.
Joy filled each home with laughter so free.
Hardships arose, but faith did abound
In homes where faith in Jesus was found.

As months quickly turned to many years,
Gatherings were filled with much cheer.
To see each face from our childhood home,
The love in our hearts did not ever roam.

Oh, what memories we all could tell,
Springing up in our hearts as a well.
Some not great and not very fond,
But all knit us together in a family bond.

Age lines now appear on each face,
But joy everlasting fills every space.
Our faith in Jesus Christ, oh such grace.
His blood washed our sin without a trace.

Loved ones have left our earthly abode.
On streets of pure gold, they now have strolled.
Awaiting our time for heavenly arrival.
Faith in Jesus is our only true survival.

God offers us love, forgiveness, and eternal life
By His only Son, Jesus, who suffered such strife
To die on the cross for our sins with His blood,
And come into our hearts and wash us like a flood.

My prayer is that we all put our trust in our Savior,
Jesus, who graciously poured on us His great favor.
Repenting of our sins and surrendering our all,
Washed by His blood, saving us from a great fall.

DONNA MCMILLIN

The lives we all have lived
To Jesus Christ we now give.
To stand together and not bend,
The road to heaven is our end.

How precious our time together has become
As we grow older, and to death someday will succumb.
Lord, teach us to number and value every day.
Let us love each other and in Jesus our Savior do not sway.

Lord God, I am so very thankful for this family You have blessed me with. My heart is so full of love and joy for them all, and I praise You, heavenly Father, that amazingly You put us all together strategically. You knew we all needed each other on this earth in all our lives. You are a wondrous Father and God. Thank You, Lord God Almighty! In Jesus's name I pray. Amen!

Behold, I stand at the door and knock. If anyone hears My voice and opens the door, I will come in to him and dine with him, and he with Me.

—Revelation 3:20

Printed in the United States
by Baker & Taylor Publisher Services